# SPSS® 11.0 Brief Guide

For more information about SPSS® software products, please visit our Web site at *http://www.spss.com* or contact

SPSS Inc.
233 South Wacker Drive, 11th Floor
Chicago, IL 60606-6412
Tel: (312) 651-3000
Fax: (312) 651-3668

SPSS® 11.0 Brief Guide
Copyright © 2001 by SPSS Inc.
Published by Prentice-Hall, Inc.
Upper Saddle River, New Jersey

Printed in the United States of America.

3 4 5 6 7 8 9 0    05 04 03 02

ISBN  0-13-034847-3

# Preface

## SPSS 11.0

SPSS 11.0 is a comprehensive system for analyzing data. SPSS can take data from almost any type of file and use them to generate tabulated reports, charts and plots of distributions and trends, descriptive statistics, and complex statistical analyses.

SPSS makes statistical analysis more accessible for the beginner and more convenient for the experienced user. Simple menus and dialog box selections make it possible to perform complex analyses without typing a single line of command syntax. The Data Editor offers a simple and efficient spreadsheet-like facility for entering data and browsing the working data file.

Interactive charts, as well as standard high-resolution charts, are included as part of the Base and Student Version systems. With interactive charts, you can explore your data by making dynamic modifications that are reflected immediately in the Viewer window. Change from bars to lines, switch variables, add error bars, separate bars into clusters, change the bins of a histogram, and modify the chart appearance, all with a few mouse clicks.

The *SPSS 11.0 Brief Guide* provides a set of tutorials designed to acquaint you with the various components of the SPSS system. You can work through the tutorials in sequence or turn to the topics for which you need additional information. Tutorials introducing interactive charts are in Chapters 6 through 8, while tutorials explaining standard charts are in Appendix A and Appendix B. You can use this book as a supplement to the online tutorial that is included with the SPSS Base 11.0 system or ignore the online tutorial and start with the tutorials found here.

### Internet Resources

The SPSS Web site (*http://www.spss.com*) offers answers to frequently asked questions about installing and running SPSS software, access to the SPSS newsletter *Keywords*, data files, and other useful information.

In addition, the SPSS USENET discussion group (not sponsored by SPSS) is open to anyone interested in SPSS products. The USENET address is *comp.soft-sys.stat.spss*. It deals with computer, statistical, and other operational issues related to SPSS software.

You can also subscribe to an e-mail message list that is gatewayed to the USENET group. To subscribe, send an e-mail message to *listserv@uga.cc.uga.edu*. The text of the e-mail message should be: subscribe SPSSX-L firstname lastname. You can then post messages to the list by sending an e-mail message to *SPSSX-L@uga.cc.uga.edu*.

## Sample Data

The data used for all but one example in this book are from a file named *Employee data.sav*. This file is included with SPSS 11.0 and the Student Version. The time series example uses a file named *Inventor.sav*. This file is included only with the Student Version.

These files are also available through the following methods:

**SPSS Web site.** You can download the files from the SPSS Web site at *http://www.spss.com/Support*. Look for the link to Datasets under Ftp Archives.

**Anonymous FTP.** The files are also available via anonymous FTP at *ftp.spss.com*. The location is *\pub\spss\sample\datasets* and the filename is *75brief.exe*.

Some data files used in the online tutorials and application examples exceed the case limit for the Student Version. For the Student Version, random samples of the original data files are provided. Results obtained with these sampled versions of the data files will differ from those shown in the online tutorials and application examples.

## Additional Publications

For additional information about the features and operations of SPSS Base 11.0, you can consult the *SPSS Base 11.0 User's Guide*, which includes information on standard graphics. Complete information about using interactive graphics can be found in *SPSS Interactive Graphics 10.0*, which is compatible with release 11.0 of SPSS. Examples using the statistical procedures found in SPSS Base 11.0 are provided in the Help system, installed with the software. Algorithms used in the statistical procedures are available on the product CD-ROM.

In addition, beneath the menus and dialog boxes, SPSS uses a command language. Some extended features of the system can be accessed only via command syntax. (Those features are not available in the Student Version.) Complete command syntax is documented in the *SPSS 11.0 Syntax Reference Guide*, provided on the product CD-ROM.

Individuals worldwide can order additional product manuals directly from the SPSS Web site at *http://www.spss.com/Pubs*. For telephone orders in the United States and Canada, call SPSS Inc. at 800-543-2185. For telephone orders outside of North America, contact your local SPSS office, listed on page viii.

Individuals in the United States can order manuals by calling Prentice Hall at 800-947-7700. If you represent a bookstore or have a Prentice Hall account, call 800-382-3419. In Canada, call 800-567-3800. Outside of North America, contact your local Prentice Hall office.

Statistical introductions to procedures in the Base, Regression Models, and Advanced Models written by Marija Norušis are planned to be available from Prentice Hall. Check with the publisher or visit the SPSS Web site for announcements regarding availability.

## SPSS Options

The following options are available as add-on enhancements to the full (not Student Version) SPSS Base system:

**SPSS Regression Models**™ provides techniques for analyzing data that do not fit traditional linear statistical models. It includes procedures for probit analysis, logistic regression, weight estimation, two-stage least-squares regression, and general nonlinear regression.

**SPSS Advanced Models**™ focuses on techniques often used in sophisticated experimental and biomedical research. It includes procedures for general linear models (GLM), linear mixed models, variance components analysis, loglinear analysis, ordinal regression, actuarial life tables, Kaplan-Meier survival analysis, and basic and extended Cox regression.

**SPSS Tables**™ creates a variety of presentation-quality tabular reports, including complex stub-and-banner tables and displays of multiple response data.

**SPSS Trends**™ performs comprehensive forecasting and time series analyses with multiple curve-fitting models, smoothing models, and methods for estimating autoregressive functions.

**SPSS Categories**® performs optimal scaling procedures, including correspondence analysis.

**SPSS Conjoint**™ performs conjoint analysis.

**SPSS Exact Tests**™ calculates exact $p$ values for statistical tests when small or very unevenly distributed samples could make the usual tests inaccurate.

**SPSS Missing Value Analysis**™ describes patterns of missing data, estimates means and other statistics, and imputes values for missing observations.

**SPSS Maps**™ turns your geographically distributed data into high-quality maps with symbols, colors, bar charts, pie charts, and combinations of themes to present not only what is happening but where it is happening.

The SPSS family of products also includes applications for data entry, text analysis, classification, neural networks, and flowcharting.

## Training Seminars

SPSS Inc. provides both public and onsite training seminars for SPSS. All seminars feature hands-on workshops. SPSS seminars will be offered in major U.S. and European cities on a regular basis. For more information on these seminars, call your local office, listed on page viii.

### Technical Support

The services of SPSS Technical Support are available to registered customers of SPSS. (Student Version customers should read the special section on technical support on page vii.) Customers may contact Technical Support for assistance in using SPSS products or for installation help for one of the supported hardware environments. To reach Technical Support, see the SPSS Web site at *http://www.spss.com*, or call your local office, listed on page viii. Be prepared to identify yourself, your organization, and the serial number of your system.

### Tell Us Your Thoughts

Your comments are important. Please let us know about your experiences with SPSS products. We especially like to hear about new and interesting applications using the SPSS system. Please send e-mail to *suggest@spss.com*, or write to SPSS Inc., Attn: Director of Product Planning, 233 South Wacker Drive, 11th Floor, Chicago IL 60606-6412.

## SPSS 11.0 for Windows Student Version

### Capability

The SPSS 11.0 for Windows Student Version is a limited but still powerful version of the SPSS 11.0 Base system. The Student Version contains all of the important data analysis tools contained in the full SPSS Base system, including:

- Spreadsheet-like Data Editor for entering, modifying, and viewing data files.
- Statistical procedures, including *t* tests, analysis of variance, crosstabulations, and multidimensional scaling.
- Interactive graphics that allow you to change or add chart elements and variables dynamically; the changes appear as soon as they are specified.
- Standard high-resolution graphics for an extensive array of analytical and presentation charts and tables.

### Limitations

Created for classroom instruction, the use of the Student Version is limited to students and instructors for educational purposes only. The Student Version does not contain all of the functions of the SPSS Base 11.0 system. The following limitations apply to the SPSS 11.0 for Windows Student Version:

- Data files cannot contain more than 50 variables.
- Data files cannot contain more than 1500 cases.

- SPSS add-on modules (such as Regression Models or Advanced Models) cannot be used with the Student Version.
- SPSS command syntax is not available to the user. This means that it is not possible to repeat an analysis by saving a series of commands in a syntax or "job" file, as can be done in the full version of SPSS.
- Scripting and automation are not available to the user. This means that you cannot create scripts that automate tasks that you repeat often, as can be done in the full version of SPSS.

## Customer Service

To report any damaged or missing components of your SPSS 11.0 for Windows Student Version, call Prentice Hall Customer Service at 800-922-0579 (800-567-3800 in Canada). Outside of the United States, contact your local Prentice Hall representative.

## Technical Support for Students

Students should obtain technical support from their instructors or from local support staff identified by their instructors. Technical support from SPSS for the SPSS 11.0 Student Version is provided *only to instructors using the system for classroom instruction.*

Before seeking assistance from your instructor, please write down the information described below. Without this information, your instructor may be unable to assist you:

- The type of PC you are using, as well as the amount of RAM and free disk space you have.
- The operating system of your PC.
- A clear description of what happened and what you were doing when the problem occurred. If possible, please try to reproduce the problem with one of the sample data files provided with the program.
- The exact wording of any error or warning messages that appeared on your screen.
- How you tried to solve the problem on your own.

## Technical Support for Instructors

Instructors using the Student Version for classroom instruction may contact SPSS Technical Support for assistance. In the United States and Canada, call SPSS Technical Support at 312-651-3410, or send an e-mail to *support@spss.com*. Please include your name, title, and academic institution.

Instructors outside of the United States and Canada should contact your local SPSS office through the SPSS home page at *http://www.spss.com*, or call your local office, listed on page viii.

SPSS Inc.
Chicago, Illinois, U.S.A.
Tel: 1.312.651.3000
or 1.800.543.2185
www.spss.com/corpinfo
**Customer Service:**
1.800.521.1337
**Sales:**
1.800.543.2185
sales@spss.com
**Training:**
1.800.543.6607
**Technical Support:**
1.312.651.3410
support@spss.com

**SPSS Federal Systems**
Tel: 1.703.740.2400
or 1.800.860.5762
www.spss.com

**SPSS Argentina srl**
Tel: +5411.4814.5030
www.spss.com

**SPSS Asia Pacific Pte. Ltd.**
Tel: +65.245.9110
www.spss.com

**SPSS Australasia Pty. Ltd.**
Tel: +61.2.9954.5660
www.spss.com

**SPSS Belgium**
Tel: +32.163.170.70
www.spss.com

**SPSS Benelux BV**
Tel: +31.183.651777
www.spss.com

**SPSS Brasil Ltda**
Tel: +55.11.5505.3644
www.spss.com

**SPSS Czech Republic**
Tel: +420.2.24813839
www.spss.cz

**SPSS Denmark**
Tel: +45.45.46.02.00
www.spss.com

**SPSS East Africa**
Tel: +254 2 577 262
spss.com

**SPSS Finland Oy**
Tel: +358.9.4355.920
www.spss.com

**SPSS France SARL**
Tel: +01.55.35.27.00
www.spss.com

**SPSS Germany**
Tel: +49.89.4890740
www.spss.com

**SPSS BI Greece**
Tel: +30.1.6971950
www.spss.com

**SPSS Iberica**
Tel: +34.902.123.606
SPSS.com

**SPSS Hong Kong Ltd.**
Tel: +852.2.811.9662
www.spss.com

**SPSS Ireland**
Tel: +353.1.415.0234
www.spss.com

**SPSS BI Israel**
Tel: +972.3.6166616
www.spss.com

**SPSS Italia srl**
Tel: +800.437300
www.spss.it

**SPSS Japan Inc.**
Tel: +81.3.5466.5511
www.spss.co.jp

**SPSS Korea DataSolution Co.**
Tel: +82.2.563.0014
www.spss.co.kr

**SPSS Latin America**
Tel: +1.312.651.3539
www.spss.com

**SPSS Malaysia Sdn Bhd**
Tel: +603.6203.2300
www.spss.com

**SPSS Miami**
Tel: 1.305.627.5700
SPSS.com

**SPSS Mexico SA de CV**
Tel: +52.5.682.87.68
www.spss.com

**SPSS Norway AS**
Tel: +47.22.99.25.50
www.spss.com

**SPSS Polska**
Tel: +48.12.6369680
www.spss.pl

**SPSS Russia**
Tel: +7.095.125.0069
www.spss.com

**SPSS San Bruno**
Tel: 1.650.794.2692
www.spss.com

**SPSS Schweiz AG**
Tel: +41.1.266.90.30
www.spss.com

**SPSS BI (Singapore) Pte. Ltd.**
Tel: +65.346.2061
www.spss.com

**SPSS South Africa**
Tel: +27.21.7120929
www.spss.com

**SPSS South Asia**
Tel: +91.80.2088069
www.spss.com

**SPSS Sweden AB**
Tel: +46.8.506.105.50
www.spss.com

**SPSS Taiwan Corp.**
Taipei, Republic of China
Tel: +886.2.25771100
www.sinter.com.tw/spss/main

**SPSS (Thailand) Co., Ltd.**
Tel: +66.2.260.7070
www.spss.com

**SPSS UK Ltd.**
Tel: +44.1483.719200
www.spss.com

# Contents

# 1

# Quick Tour

This tour provides a quick preview of SPSS. More detailed information is available in later chapters and in the online Help system. The following techniques are briefly demonstrated:

- Starting and exiting from SPSS
- Opening a data file in the Data Editor
- Using the Analyze menu to obtain a frequency table and bar chart
- Viewing output
- Getting information from online Help and the online tutorial

## Online Tutorial

The online tutorial, which is part of the Help that is installed with the software, provides an overview. While the online tutorial lacks the "hands-on" approach of the tutorials in this manual, it provides a more complete introduction to a number of features, such as the toolbar. (Other topics, such as data transformations, are covered more extensively in the manual.)

The tutorial can be accessed from any window. (See "Getting Started" on p. 2 for details on starting the software.) To start the tutorial, choose Tutorial from the Help menu. This opens the Contents tab, as shown in Figure 1.1.

**Figure 1.1    Help topics: Online tutorial**

*If SPSS is already running, you can run the tutorial by choosing Tutorial from the Help menu.*

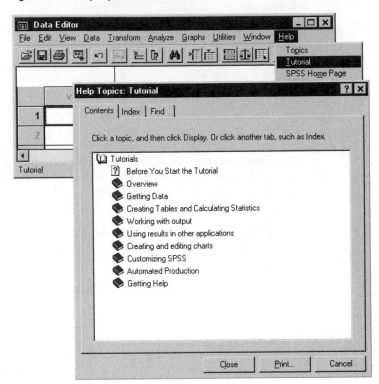

The Contents tab is organized by topic, like a table of contents. Double-click on items with a book icon to expand or collapse the contents. Double-click on an item to go to that Help topic.

## Getting Started

To start a session:

① From the Programs submenu on the Windows Start menu, select SPSS 11.0 for Windows Student Version or choose the SPSS for Windows program group.

② Then choose SPSS 11.0 for Windows.

**Figure 1.2 Starting SPSS for Windows**

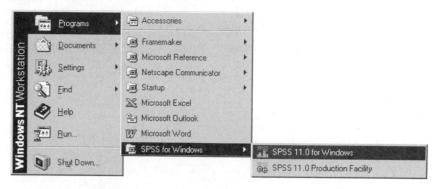

This opens the Data Editor window, as shown in Figure 1.3.

**Figure 1.3 Data Editor window**

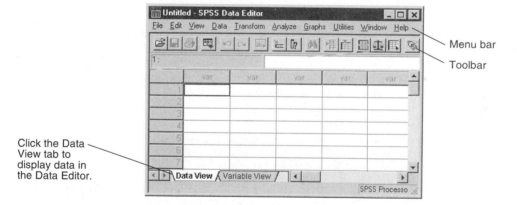

Menu bar

Toolbar

Click the Data View tab to display data in the Data Editor.

## Opening a Data File

For this example, the data are in a file named *Employee data.sav.* (See the preface if you don't find this file on your system or Chapter 4 if you need more information about opening a data file.)

❶ Click File on the menu bar.

❷ Click Open.

❸ Click Data.

This opens the Open File dialog box, as shown in Figure 1.4.

**Figure 1.4    Opening a previously saved data file**

List of files

File Name
text box

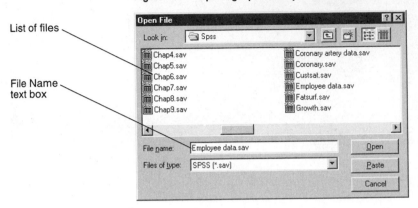

④ Select *Employee data.sav* on the list.

*Another way to open a file is to double-click on the filename on the list.*

This enters the name of the file in the File Name text box.

⑤ Click Open.

This opens the data file. The Data Editor window, containing data from *Employee data.sav*, is shown in Figure 1.5.

**Figure 1.5    Data Editor window**

Cases

Switch between Data View and Variable View by clicking these tabs. Variable View will be discussed in Chapter 3.

Variables

Click here to scroll through data.

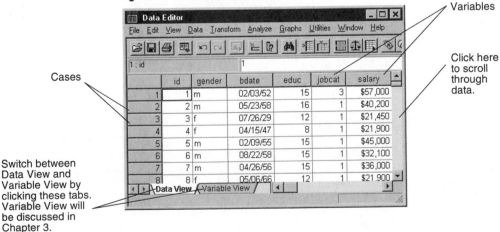

*Some variables use numeric codes for categories. For the variable minority, 0 is a code for "no" and 1 is a code for "yes."*

At the top of the Data Editor is a row of names for the types of information included in the columns of the data file. These are called **variables**. The first variable, *Employee Code*, indicates that the numbers in the first column represent ID numbers for employees. Five columns to the right, the variable *Current Salary* indicates that the column contains the annual salary for each employee.

The rows in the data file are called **cases**. In this file, each of 474 cases contains the data for one employee.

## Calculating Simple Statistics

*To see the names of the job categories, switch to Variable View by clicking the tab at the bottom of the window. Then select the Values cell for Employment Category and click the ... button.*

Now that you have a data file open, you can calculate some simple statistics. When you first start to analyze a set of data, you often want to know how many cases are in various categories. The Frequencies procedure does the counting for you and displays the results in a table.

The variable *Employment Category* contains codes for employee job categories. Each type of job is coded with a number from 1 to 3. A label for each of the code numbers is stored in the data file, and these labels are used when displaying the results.

❶ To calculate how many cases are in specified categories, from the menus choose:

Analyze
  Descriptive Statistics
    Frequencies...

Figure 1.6 shows the Analyze menu and Descriptive Statistics submenu.

**Figure 1.6    Choosing a statistical procedure**

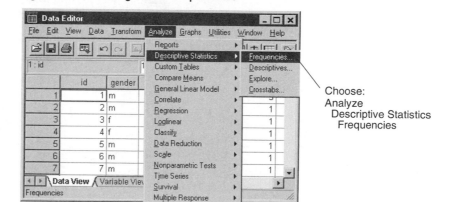

Choosing the Frequencies procedure from the menus opens the Frequencies dialog box, as shown in Figure 1.7. The Frequencies procedure counts the number of cases in various categories.

**Figure 1.7    Selecting variables**

Click here
to move Employment
Category.

List of available
variables

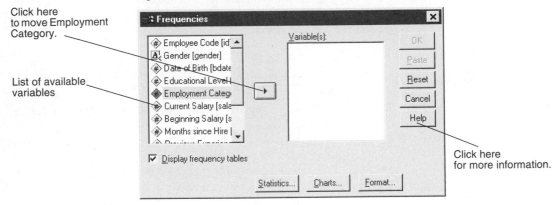

Click here
for more information.

The variables available in the *Employee data.sav* data file are listed on the left.

*You can double-click on Employment Category to move it to the Variable(s) list.*

**❷** Select *Employment Category* and then click the arrow button.

This moves *Employment Category* to the Variable(s) list. Be sure you select the *Employment Category* variable. If you select *Employee Code*, you will have an enormous frequencies table.

At this point, look at the Help facility for information about what to do next. When you are learning something new, click Help whenever you need assistance.

**❸** Click Help in the dialog box.

This opens a window containing information about the current dialog box, Frequencies, as shown in Figure 1.8.

**Figure 1.8    Frequencies Help**

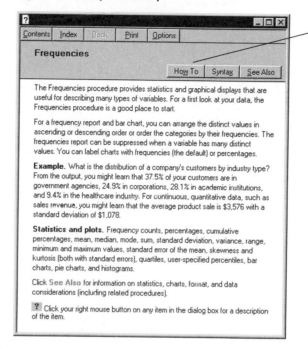

Click here to find out how to use the dialog box to run the procedure.

④ To exit from the Help window, click the X button in the upper right corner of the Help window.

This returns you to the Frequencies dialog box.

⑤ Click Charts to open the Frequencies Charts dialog box, as shown in Figure 1.9.

**Figure 1.9    Selecting a chart type**

Click here to create a bar chart.

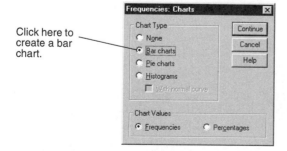

**6** Select Bar charts.

**7** Click Continue.

This closes the Frequencies Charts dialog box.

**8** In the Frequencies dialog box, click OK.

The results are displayed in the Viewer window.

**Figure 1.10    Viewer window**

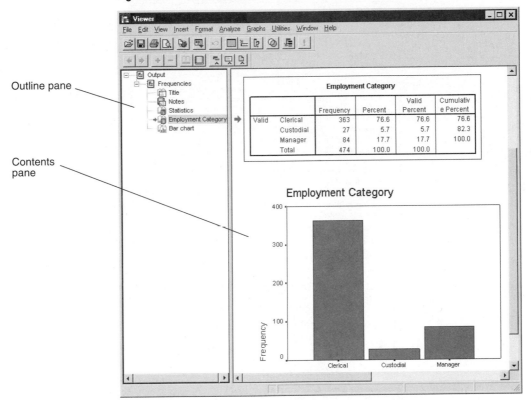

Outline pane

Contents pane

## Viewing the Output

The Viewer contains an outline pane and a contents pane. You can view different parts of your output by using the scroll bars in the contents pane or by clicking the item you want to view in the outline pane.

## Experimenting with Other Procedures

If you want to try some other procedures, go ahead and experiment now. For example, you could click on the Analyze menu and select Descriptive Statistics and then Descriptives to display summary statistics and calculate standardized values. After the dialog box opens, select the variables *Beginning Salary* and *Current Salary*.

If you aren't sure how the descriptive statistics are defined, click Options in the Descriptives dialog box. Then, click your right mouse button on any statistic you don't recognize and a definition will pop up.

Click OK in the Descriptives dialog box to run the Descriptives procedure.

## Ending the SPSS Session

❶ To exit SPSS, from the menus choose:

File
  Exit

as shown in Figure 1.11.

**Figure 1.11     Exiting SPSS**

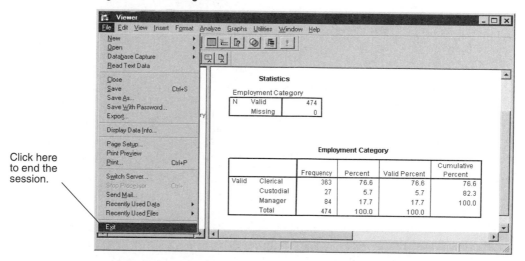

You are then asked if you want to save the contents of the Viewer.

❷ Click No.

This ends the session.

## Should I Save the Data File?

For these tutorials, when you are asked if you want to save the data file, click No. This will happen only if you changed something in the data file, such as a data value, a variable name, or the order of the cases. When you use a file and see it in the Data Editor, the actual copy on the disk is not changed. The disk file is changed only if you save the file. Since the *Employee data.sav* file will be used in its original form in the next few chapters, it should not be changed.

# What's Next?

The tutorials in the following chapters allow you to explore SPSS in greater depth, continuing the hands-on approach used in this quick tour. In addition, brief information on the basics of running selected statistical procedures is presented in the last section of this book. For detailed information on statistical procedures, consult a statistics or data analysis textbook.

The online tutorial provides a more complete introduction to a number of features, such as the toolbar. (See "Online Tutorial" on p. 1.)

For the most complete coverage of SPSS, consult the online Help system. Chapter 2 provides an introduction to Help.

# 2 Tutorial: Using the Help System

The Help system provides the information that you need to use SPSS and understand the results. This tutorial demonstrates the following:

- Using the Statistics Coach
- Locating topics in the Help contents
- Searching the Help index for a specified topic

This tutorial can be done with any open data file (such as *Employee data.sav*).

## Using the Statistics Coach

If you are not familiar with SPSS or with the available statistical procedures, the Statistics Coach can help you get started with many of the basic statistical techniques in the SPSS Base system. Suppose you want to see whether there is a relationship between beginning salary and current salary. To figure out what statistical procedure to use, you can consult the Statistics Coach.

*Note*: The Statistic Coach uses components of Internet Explorer. The SPSS installation CD provides both an upgrade to Internet Explorer 4 and a fully installable version of Internet Explorer 5.

Before starting the Statistics Coach, open a file such as *Employee data.sav*.

❶ From the menus choose:

Help
 Statistics Coach

**Figure 2.1    Statistics Coach**

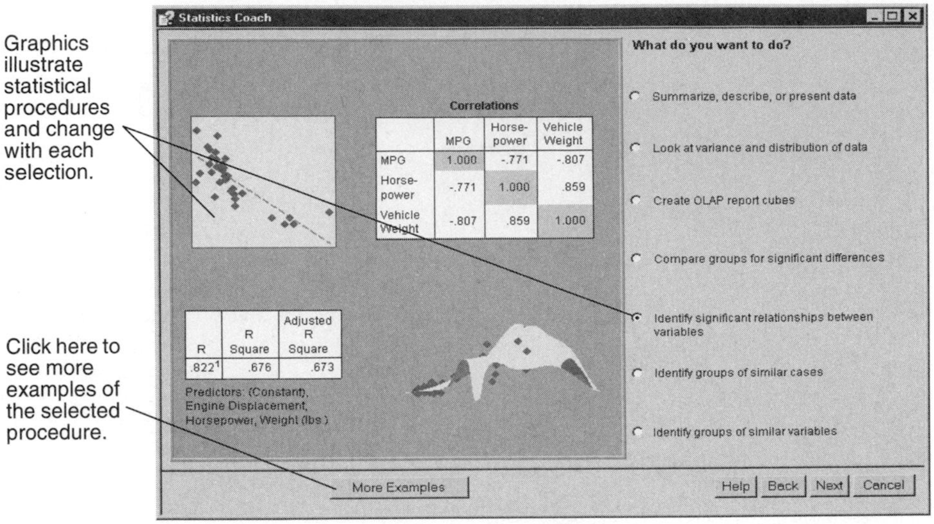

Graphics illustrate statistical procedures and change with each selection.

Click here to see more examples of the selected procedure.

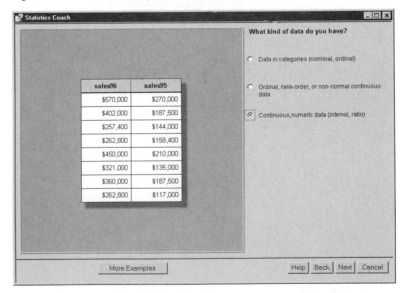

❷ Since we want to see if there is a relationship between two variables, select Identify significant relationships between variables and click Next.

**Figure 2.2    Determine the type of data you have**

❸ Since salaries are continuous data, select Continuous, numeric data (interval, ratio).

❹ Click Next.

**Figure 2.3    Determine the number of variables to evaluate**

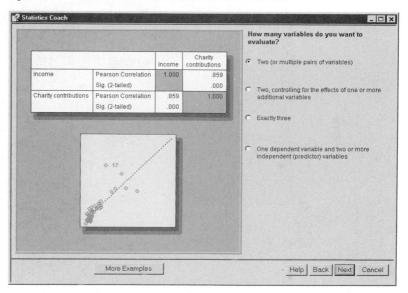

❺ Since we want to compare two variables, *beginning salary* and *current salary*, select Two (or multiple pairs of variables) and click Next.

**Figure 2.4    Statistics Coach showing statistical output**

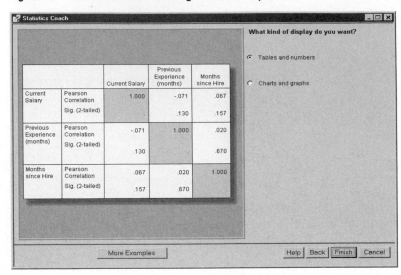

⑥ If you are interested in statistical output rather than charts and graphs, select Tables and numbers and click Finish.

After you click Finish, a dialog box for the Bivariate Correlations procedure is displayed as well as a Help topic on obtaining Pearson correlations.

**Figure 2.5    Statistics Coach leads to the appropriate statistical procedure**

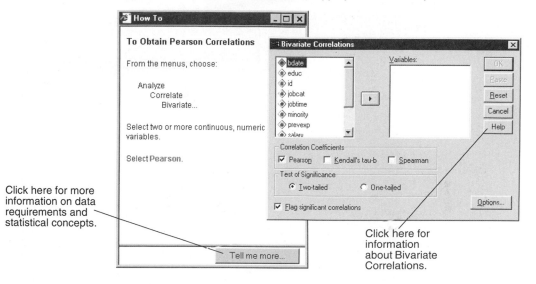

Click here for more information on data requirements and statistical concepts.

Click here for information about Bivariate Correlations.

❼ View a correlations table by completing the Bivariate Correlations dialog box. Then click OK.

❽ You can also learn more about data requirements by clicking Tell me more.

## Locating Topics in the Help Contents

Suppose that you want to make a chart of your data. You have a picture in mind of what the chart should look like, but you are unsure of what it is called or whether it is available. To find out, you can consult the Help system, as illustrated in the following steps:

❶ From the menus choose:

Help
  Topics

*You can also access Help by clicking the Help button in any dialog box. Information about that dialog box will automatically be displayed.*

❷ Click the Contents tab.

This opens the Help Contents window, as shown in Figure 2.6. (You can always return to this window from anywhere in Help by clicking the Contents button near the top of a Help window.)

**Figure 2.6    Help system Contents tab**

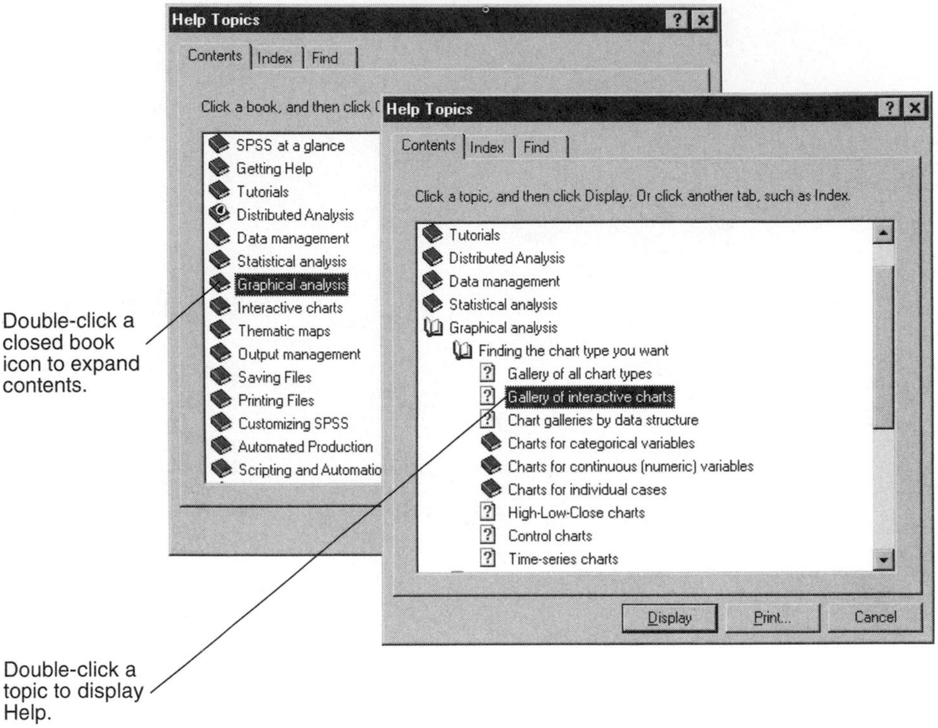

Double-click a
closed book
icon to expand
contents.

Double-click a
topic to display
Help.

❸ Double-click the closed book icon for Graphical analysis.

❹ Double-click the closed book icon for Finding the chart type you want.

Double-clicking book icons in the Contents tab expands and collapses the displayed list of topics.

❺ Double-click the topic Gallery of interactive charts.

This takes you to a window displaying icons for all of the interactive chart types (see Figure 2.7). *Note*: To view the gallery for standard charts, in step 5 above double-click the topic Gallery of all chart types.

**Figure 2.7      Interactive chart types**

Click here
for the
histogram
gallery.

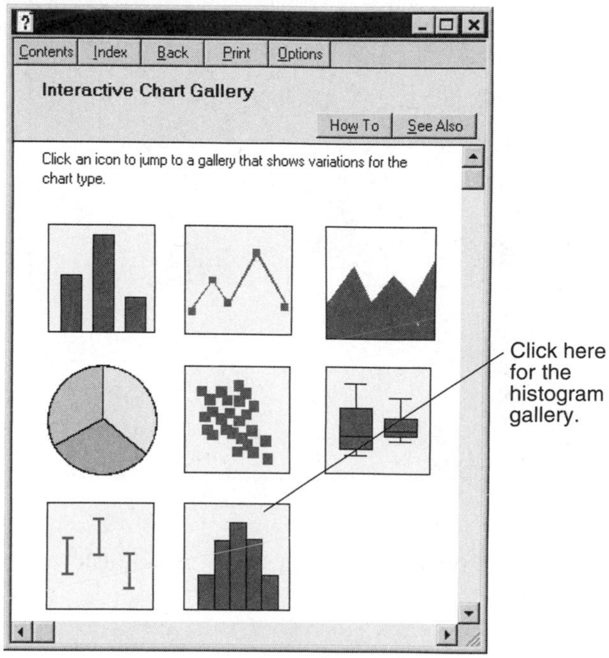

**❻** Click the histogram icon, as shown in Figure 2.7.

This opens the Histogram Gallery, as shown in Figure 2.8.

**Figure 2.8    Histogram gallery**

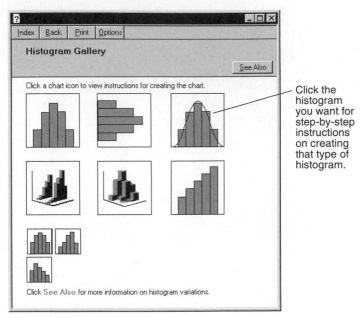

Click the histogram you want for step-by-step instructions on creating that type of histogram.

❼ Click the type of histogram you want to create, as shown in Figure 2.8.

Another Help window displays step-by-step instructions for creating an interactive histogram, as shown in Figure 2.9.

**Figure 2.9    Information on creating interactive histograms**

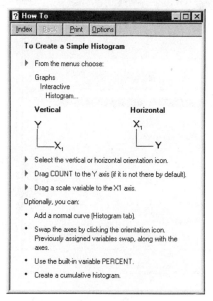

## Searching the Help Index

Rather than using the Help Contents tab, you can often find the information you want more quickly by using Help's search feature. For example, suppose that you want to find out how to calculate percentiles and you do not find percentiles on the statistics menus.

**1** From the menus choose:

Help
  Topics

❷ Click the Index tab.

**Figure 2.10    Help system Index tab**

*Another way to open the Index tab is to click the Index button in a Help window.*

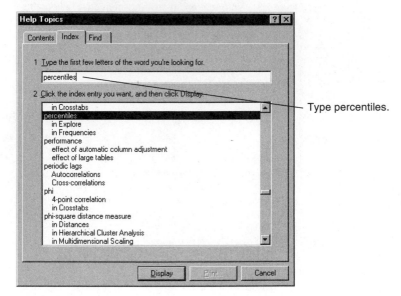

The window opens with the cursor in the text box.

❸ Type **percentiles** in the text box.

The list scrolls until percentiles is highlighted.

Several topics are listed under percentiles.

❹ Double-click the topic labeled in Frequencies.

This opens a Help window that gives you information about statistics available for the Frequencies procedure, as shown in Figure 2.11.

**Figure 2.11    Information about Frequencies statistics**

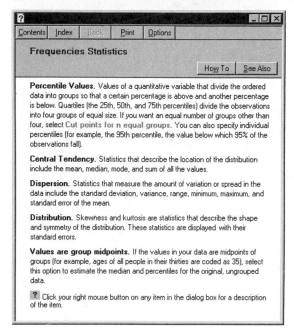

## Searching the Interactive Charts Index

Help for interactive graphics is located in a separate Help file. The following steps illustrate how to get to the Help index for interactive charts.

❶ From the SPSS menus choose:

Graphs
  Interactive

❷ Select any type of interactive chart. For example, select Bar.

❸ In the Create Bar Chart dialog box, click Help.

**Figure 2.12    Create Bar Chart dialog box**

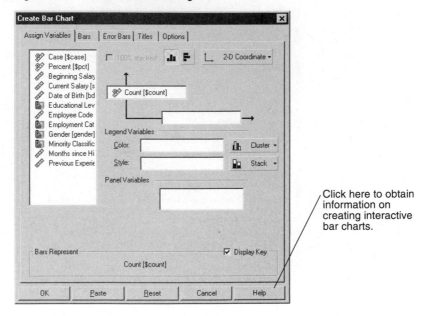

Click here to obtain information on creating interactive bar charts.

This opens a Help window that gives you information about creating a bar chart.

**Figure 2.13    Information about creating an interactive bar chart**

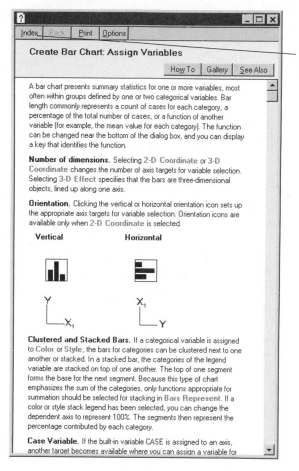

Click here to obtain the interactive charts index.

❹ Click the Index button to display the interactive charts index. This index should start with 3-D charts.

**Figure 2.14    Interactive charts index**

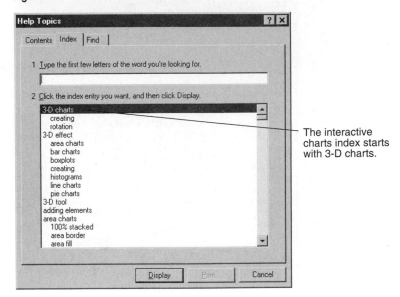

The interactive charts index starts with 3-D charts.

❺ To view information about colors in interactive charts, type **colors** in the text box and click Display.

**Figure 2.15    Interactive charts index**

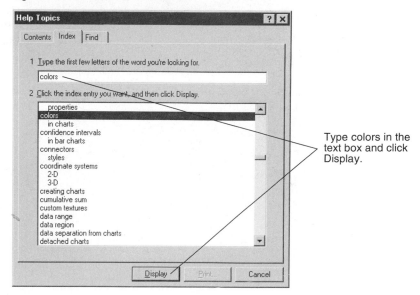

Type colors in the text box and click Display.

This brings up the topic Colors in Charts, as shown in Figure 2.16.

**Figure 2.16    Information about colors in interactive charts**

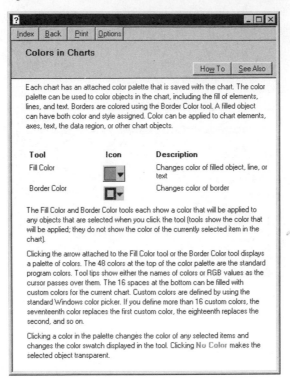

## How to Ask for Help

You can ask for help in any of the following ways:

- Click the Help button in any dialog box for information about that dialog box.

- From the menu bar, open the Help menu and select a topic.

- From the Help menu, open the Statistics Coach to get started with many basic statistical procedures.

- Click your right mouse button on any control in most dialog boxes for a pop-up explanation of what the control does (see Figure 2.17).

- Activate a pivot table and select Results Coach from the Help menu (see Chapter 4).

*Click the Help button in any dialog box for information about that dialog box.*

- Click your right mouse button on a label in an activated pivot table and select What's This? from the context menu for a pop-up definition of the term.

**Figure 2.17    Pop-up definitions with right mouse button**

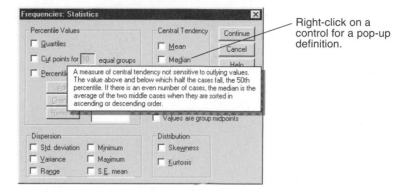

Right-click on a control for a pop-up definition.

## What's Next?

At this point, you can exit SPSS. If you have changed the data file in any way, you will be asked whether you want to save the changes. Do *not* save changes to the *Employee data.sav* data file.

If you want to try some more statistics, brief tutorials for selected procedures are provided in Chapter 14.

# 3 Tutorial: Using the Data Editor

This tutorial introduces the use of the Data Editor and demonstrates the following:

- Entering data in the Data Editor
- Naming variables
- Defining a string variable
- Defining value labels for a variable
- Saving data files

When you start an SPSS session, the Data Editor window automatically opens, as shown in Figure 3.1. (See Chapter 1 if you do not know how to start the software.)

**Figure 3.1    Data Editor in Data view**

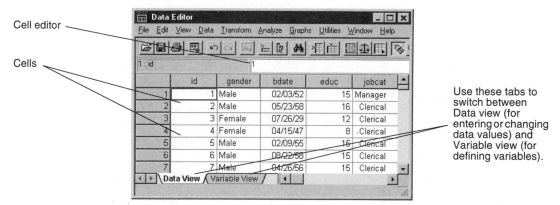

Cell editor

Cells

Use these tabs to switch between Data view (for entering or changing data values) and Variable view (for defining variables).

The Data Editor provides a convenient spreadsheet-like facility for entering, editing, and displaying the contents of your data file. If you open a previously saved data file, you can use the Data Editor to change data values and add or delete cases and variables.

The Data Editor provides two views of your data:

- **Data View.** Displays the actual data values or defined value labels. You can also use the Data Editor to enter data and create a data file. See Figure 3.1 for an example of the Data Editor in Data view.

- **Variable View.** Displays variable definition information, such as variable and value labels, data type (string, date, or numeric), and measurement scale (nominal, ordinal, or scale), as shown in Figure 3.2.

In both views, you can add, change, and delete information contained in the data file.

**Figure 3.2    Data Editor in Variable view**

To change the data type for a variable, select the appropriate cell and click here to select a data type from the dialog box.

Click this tab to return to Data view.

You can also use Variable view to change variable labels. Simply type a new label in the cell.

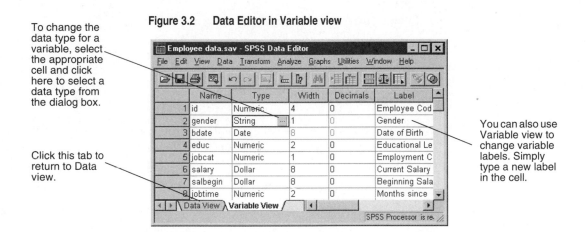

## Entering Data

You can enter data, such as numbers, directly in the Data Editor. In Data view, simply type the number in the appropriate cell and press Enter. For example, you could enter the age for the students in your class:

**❶** If you are not already in Data view, click the **Data View** tab at the bottom of the window.

**❷** Click on the first cell in the Data Editor (top left corner) and type **21**.

The number also appears in the cell editor at the top of the Data Editor as you enter it.

By entering data in the cell, you automatically create a variable with the default name *var00001*, which is displayed at the top of the column. (Replacing default variable names is discussed on p. 31. Variable naming rules are listed on p. 36.)

**③** Continue entering values in the first column:

**19** (press Enter)
**22** (press Enter)
(skip this cell; do not enter a value)
**22** (press Enter)
**20** (press Enter)
**19** (press Enter)

The Data Editor should now look like Figure 3.3.

**Figure 3.3    Data Editor after entering data**

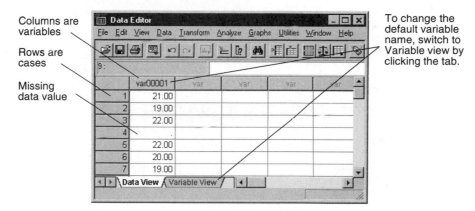

Columns are variables

Rows are cases

Missing data value

To change the default variable name, switch to Variable view by clicking the tab.

A period is displayed in the cell that does not have a data value. The period represents the **system-missing value**. In this example, it could be a person in the class who did not want to reveal his or her age.

## Naming Variables

*The variable names NewVar, newvar, and NEWVAR are considered identical.*

To replace the default variable name with a more descriptive variable name:

**①** You first need to switch to Variable view. Double-click the variable name *var00001* at the top of the first column to open the data file in Variable view, or click the Variable View tab at the bottom of the Data Editor window.

**②** Select the cell with the default variable name *var00001* and type **age**.

The variable name is automatically replaced. If you switch back to Data view by clicking the tab, you can see that the variable name *age* is now displayed at the top of the first column in the Data Editor.

# Defining Variables

Using Variable view, you can change variable definition information, such as variable labels and variable type. When working with names, dates, and other non-numeric data, you need to define the variable type before entering your data. To define the variable type for a new variable:

❶ Click the Variable View tab or double-click at the top of the second column of the Data Editor (to the right of the column of numbers you entered earlier).

❷ You can give the new variable a name by typing **gender** in the *Name* cell.

❸ Click the button in the *Type* cell for the new variable.

This opens the Variable Type dialog box, as shown in Figure 3.4.

**Figure 3.4    Variable Type dialog box**

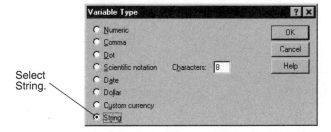

❹ Select String in the Variable Type dialog box and click OK.

The variable *gender* is now known as a **string variable**. A string variable can contain both letters and numbers.

## Adding Value Labels

In Variable view, you can assign descriptive value labels for each value of a variable. Value labels make it easier to interpret your data, charts, and statistical results.

❶ Click the button in the *Values* cell for the gender variable.

This opens the Value Labels dialog box, as shown in Figure 3.5.

**Figure 3.5    Value Labels dialog box**

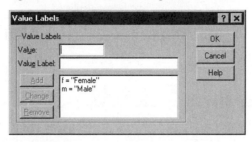

**2** Type **m** in the Value text box.

**3** Type **Male** in the Value Label text box.

**4** Click Add.

**5** Go back and type **f** in the Value text box.

**6** Type **Female** in the Value Label text box.

**7** Click Add, and then click OK to return to Variable view.

*String data values are case sensitive. A value label assigned to m will not be used for data entered as M.*

You can now use the single letter codes **m** and **f** (lower case in this example) for data entry, and the more descriptive value labels, *Male* and *Female*, will be displayed in statistical output and charts. Note that string values are case sensitive. This means that using the uppercase **M** and **F** will not assign the value labels *Male* and *Female*.

**8** In order to enter gender data, you need to switch to Data view (click the Data View tab).

**9** In the column for the string variable *gender*, type the following:

**m** (press Enter)
**m** (press Enter)
**f** (press Enter)
**m** (press enter)
**f** (press Enter)
**f** (press Enter)
**m** (press Enter)

*You can also display value labels by clicking*

**10** From the menus choose:

View
  Value Labels

The value labels for *gender* are now displayed in the Data Editor, as shown in Figure 3.6. If you click on any cell in the column for the variable *gender*, the actual value will be displayed in the cell editor at the top of the Data Editor window.

**Figure 3.6    Data Editor with value labels displayed**

*You can open a window summarizing variable definition information by clicking*

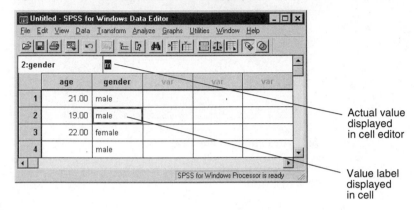

## Saving a Data File

If you want to save the data file:

❶ Make the Data Editor the active window (click anywhere in the Data Editor).

❷ From the menus choose:

File
  Save As...

This opens the Save Data As dialog box, as shown in Figure 3.7.

**Figure 3.7    Save Data As dialog box**

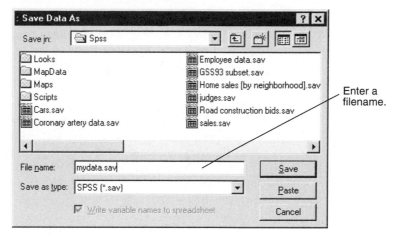

Enter a
filename.

❸ Enter a name for the data file in the File Name text box and click Save to save
the data file.

By default, data files are saved in SPSS format. For information on saving (or
reading) data files in other formats, see Chapter 11.

# Additional Information

The following sections provide additional information that you might find
useful.

## Moving Variables in the Data Editor

You can rearrange variables in the Data Editor using the drag-and-drop method:

❶ Click the variable name in Data view or the row number for the variable in
Variable view to select the variable.

❷ Drag and drop the variable to the new location.

❸ If you want to place the variable between two existing variables, in Data view
drop the variable on the variable column to the right of where you want to place
the variable. In Variable view, drop it on the variable row below where you
want to place the variable.

## Missing Values

The data you want to use for analysis may not always contain complete information for every case. For example, some respondents may refuse to answer a certain survey question. There are two methods for handling missing values.

- **System-missing value.** If no value is entered for a numeric variable, the system-missing value (represented by a period in the Data Editor) is assigned.
- **User-missing values.** Data can be missing for a variety of reasons. If you know why particular data are missing, you can assign values that identify information missing for specific reasons and then flag these values as missing. To define user-missing values, switch to Variable view and scroll to the *Missing* column. Select the desired cell and click the button to open the Missing Values dialog box. Then enter the values or range of values that represent missing data.

## Variable Naming Rules

The basic rules for variable names (not variable labels) are:
- The name must begin with a letter.
- Variable names cannot end with a period.
- The length of the variable name cannot exceed eight characters.
- Variable names cannot contain blanks or special characters (for example, !, ?, ', and *).
- Each variable name must be unique. Duplication is not allowed.
- Variable names are not case sensitive.

# What's Next?

At this point, you can exit the program or continue with the next tutorial.

# 4 Working with Statistics

This chapter introduces the use of the Analyze menu and demonstrates the following:

- Opening a data file in the Data Editor
- Obtaining a crosstabulation of two variables
- Finding information about results and variables

## Opening a Data File

SPSS is able to open a number of different types of data files, including spreadsheet files created with Lotus 1-2-3, Excel, and Multiplan, dBASE files, tab-delimited ASCII files, and SYSTAT data files. This tutorial uses the data file *Employee data.sav*.

❶ To open the *Employee data.sav* data file, from the menus choose:

File
  Open
    Data...

This opens the Open File dialog box, as shown in Figure 4.1.

**Figure 4.1    Open File dialog box**

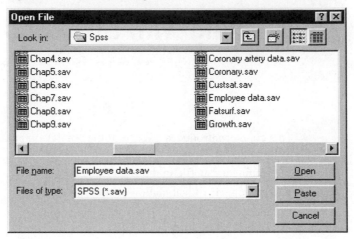

*If you can't find the data file, make sure that you are looking in the directory where SPSS is installed (usually c:\program files\spss) and that files with the .sav extension are listed.*

❷ Select *Employee data.sav* in the list of files.

❸ Click Open or press Enter.

The data file is displayed in the Data Editor window, as shown in Figure 4.2. The appearance of the data file varies depending on whether or not value labels are displayed.

*You can display (or hide) value labels by clicking*

**Figure 4.2    Data Editor windows (with and without value labels displayed)**

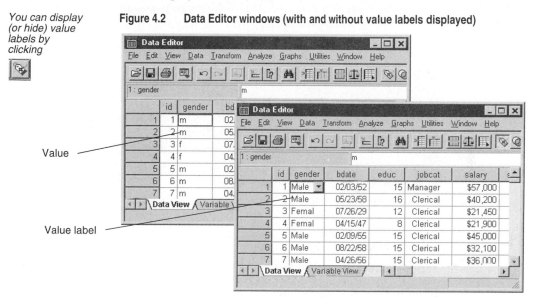

Value

Value label

## The Employee Data File

The file *Employee data.sav* contains historical data about a company's employees. The data were gathered as part of a study to determine whether the company had discriminated against women and minorities in its employment practices. The file contains the following variables:

*Variables such as minority and employment category use numeric codes to represent categorical information.*

- *id*—the employee's identification number (in order of hiring).
- *gender* —coded as follows: m=male, f=female.
- *minority*—the employee's minority status: 0=no, 1=yes.
- *bdate*—the date of birth for each employee.
- *educ*—the highest grade level completed by the employee: 12=high school diploma, 16=bachelor's degree, and so on.

*Variables such as jobtime and salary represent actual numerical data.*

- *jobcat*—the individual's employment category: 1=clerical, 2=custodial, 3=manager.
- *salary*—the employee's current salary, adjusted to 1992 dollars.
- *salbegin*—the employee's salary at time of hiring, in 1992 dollars.

- *jobtime*—the number of months the employee has been with the company.
- *prevexp*—employee's experience (in months) prior to joining the company.

**Variable labels.** To see the variable label for a variable, hold your mouse pointer over the variable name in Data view.

## Using Statistical Procedures

The Analyze menu contains a list of general statistical categories. The arrow (▶) following each menu selection indicates that there is an additional menu level. The individual statistical procedures are listed at this submenu level.

To examine the relationship between job category, gender, and minority among company employees, you can crosstabulate the variables *Employment Category* and *Gender* within categories of *Minority Classification*.

❶ To obtain a crosstabulation, from the menus choose:

Analyze
 Descriptive Statistics
  Crosstabs...

This opens the Crosstabs dialog box, as shown in Figure 4.3.

**Figure 4.3    Crosstabs dialog box**

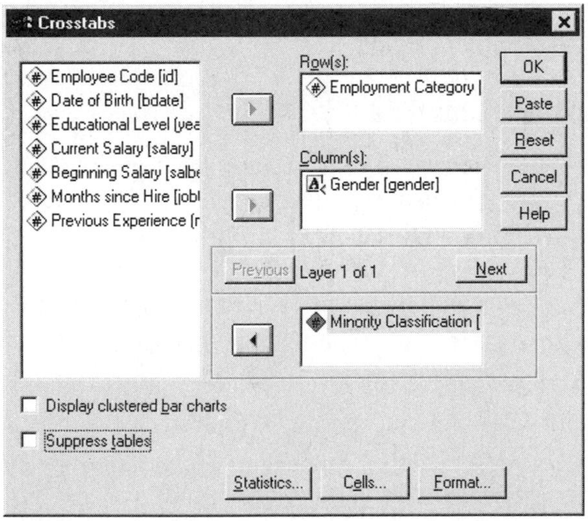

*You can directly access variable information from most dialog boxes. Simply click on any variable with the right mouse button and then select Variable Information from the resulting menu.*

❷ Select *Employment Category* on the variable list and click the arrow button next to the Row(s) list.

This moves *Employment Category* to the Row(s) list.

❸ Select *Gender* on the variable list and click the arrow button next to the Column(s) list.

This moves *Gender* to the Column(s) list.

❹ Select *Minority Classification* on the variable list and click the arrow button next to the Layer list.

This moves *Minority Classification* to the Layer list. The dialog box should appear as shown in Figure 4.3 above.

❺ Click OK.

This closes the dialog box and runs the procedure.

The results—a crosstabulation for *Employment Category* and *Gender* within categories of *Minority Classification*—are displayed in the Viewer window, as shown in Figure 4.4.

**Figure 4.4    Crosstabulation displayed in Viewer**

*You can use the maximize button and scroll bars to see more of the output.*

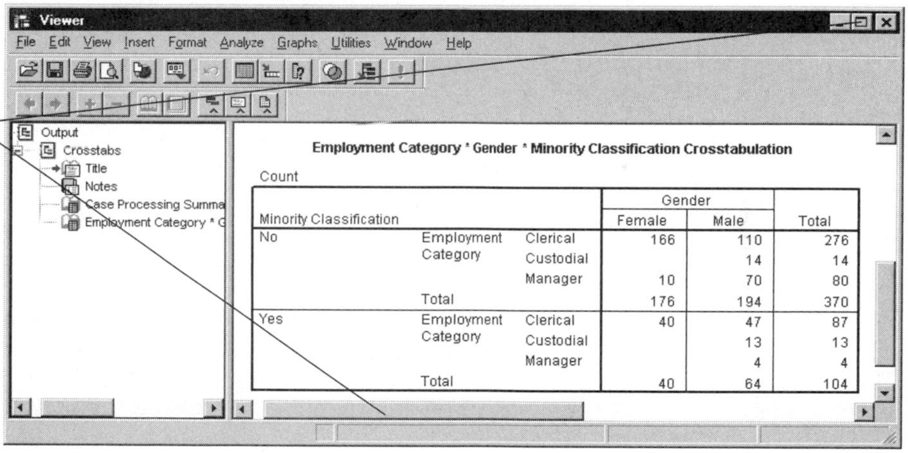

**Employment Category * Gender * Minority Classification Crosstabulation**

Count

| Minority Classification | | | Gender | | Total |
|---|---|---|---|---|---|
| | | | Female | Male | |
| No | Employment Category | Clerical | 166 | 110 | 276 |
| | | Custodial | | 14 | 14 |
| | | Manager | 10 | 70 | 80 |
| | Total | | 176 | 194 | 370 |
| Yes | Employment Category | Clerical | 40 | 47 | 87 |
| | | Custodial | | 13 | 13 |
| | | Manager | | 4 | 4 |
| | Total | | 40 | 64 | 104 |

## Using the Results Coach

The Results Coach provides information to help you interpret tables in the Viewer.

To use the Results Coach:

❶ Right-click anywhere in the table and select Results Coach from the menu.

This displays a Help topic that provides information about your table.

**②** Click the Next button twice to display the information shown in Figure 4.5.

Figure 4.5    Results Coach

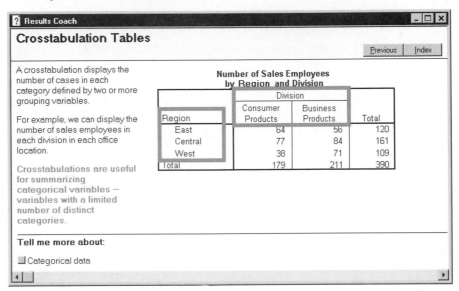

## Running Procedures with Additional Specifications

While running a procedure, you can request additional specifications in subdialog boxes, which are accessed from the main dialog box.

In the output from the previous crosstabulation, the distribution of gender and minority does not appear to be equal across different job categories. Most women (and *all* minority women) are clerical workers, while a large majority of managers are nonminority males. This suggests that there is a relationship between the variables *Gender, Minority Classification,* and *Employment Category.* But what is this relationship? And is it statistically significant?

To more closely examine the distribution of *Gender* and *Minority Classification* across each value of *Employment Category*, you can repeat the above crosstabulation, using an additional specification to display expected counts in each cell.

*You can also reopen the dialog box by clicking on the Dialog Recall button*

① To obtain a crosstabulation with expected counts displayed in each cell, from the menus choose:

Analyze
  Descriptive Statistics
    Crosstabs...

This reopens the Crosstabs dialog box, as shown in Figure 4.3 on p. 40. (Notice that your previous selections have persisted.)

② Move the variable *Employment Category* to the Row(s) list if it is not already there.

③ Move *Gender* to the Column(s) list if it is not already there.

④ Move *Minority Classification* to the Layer list if it is not already there.

⑤ Click Cells in the Crosstabs dialog box.

This opens the Crosstabs Cell Display dialog box, as shown in Figure 4.6.

**Figure 4.6    Crosstabs Cell Display dialog box**

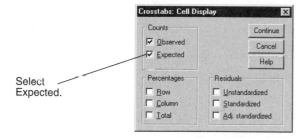

Select Expected.

⑥ Select Expected in the Counts group.

Expected counts will be displayed in each cell of the crosstabulation. The **expected count** is the number of observations that would occur in each cell if there were no relationship between the variables.

⑦ Click Continue to close the Crosstabs Cell Display dialog box and return to the main Crosstabs dialog box.

⑧ Click OK to run the procedure.

The results are displayed in the Viewer window, as shown in Figure 4.7.

**Figure 4.7 Crosstabulation with expected percentages**

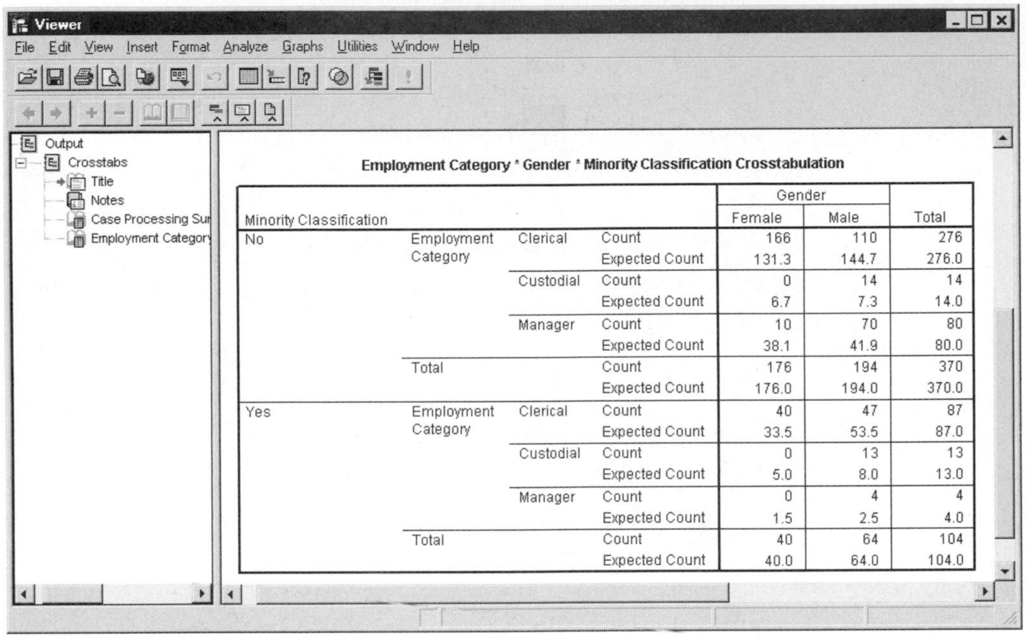


**Employment Category * Gender * Minority Classification Crosstabulation**

| Minority Classification | | | | Gender: Female | Gender: Male | Total |
|---|---|---|---|---|---|---|
| No | Employment Category | Clerical | Count | 166 | 110 | 276 |
| | | | Expected Count | 131.3 | 144.7 | 276.0 |
| | | Custodial | Count | 0 | 14 | 14 |
| | | | Expected Count | 6.7 | 7.3 | 14.0 |
| | | Manager | Count | 10 | 70 | 80 |
| | | | Expected Count | 38.1 | 41.9 | 80.0 |
| | Total | | Count | 176 | 194 | 370 |
| | | | Expected Count | 176.0 | 194.0 | 370.0 |
| Yes | Employment Category | Clerical | Count | 40 | 47 | 87 |
| | | | Expected Count | 33.5 | 53.5 | 87.0 |
| | | Custodial | Count | 0 | 13 | 13 |
| | | | Expected Count | 5.0 | 8.0 | 13.0 |
| | | Manager | Count | 0 | 4 | 4 |
| | | | Expected Count | 1.5 | 2.5 | 4.0 |
| | Total | | Count | 40 | 64 | 104 |
| | | | Expected Count | 40.0 | 64.0 | 104.0 |

The expected cell counts provide further indication that jobs may be unequally distributed across gender and minority categories. For example, there are almost twice as many nonminority males in salaried positions as you would expect if the variables were unrelated. The actual count is 70, while the expected count is only 41.9. Conversely, the expected number of minority females in clerical jobs is only 33.5, while the actual number is 40.

While the above crosstabulation suggests that a relationship does indeed exist between the variables, this analysis falls short of demonstrating that it is statistically significant.

## Finding Information about Variables

There are several ways to easily keep track of variable definition information.

- In most dialog boxes, click on any listed variable name with the *right* mouse button; then select Variable Information from the menu to pop up a window displaying any variable and value labels defined for that variable.

- For complete information about all of the variables in the current data file, choose Variables from the Utilities menu. This opens the Variables window, as shown in Figure 4.8. For further instructions, click Help in the Variables window.

**Figure 4.8    Variables window**

*You can also open the Variables window by clicking*

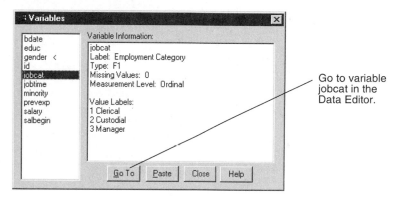

Go to variable jobcat in the Data Editor.

## What's Next?

At this point, you can exit or continue with the next tutorial. If you exit and you have changed the data file in any way, you will be asked whether you want to save the changes. Do *not* save changes to the *Employee data.sav* data file.

# 5 Working with Output

Data analysis frequently requires numerous preliminary, exploratory steps, and many statistical procedures can generate a large volume of output. There are a number of facilities to help you navigate, edit, and save your results. This tutorial introduces you to the use of the Viewer and the Draft Viewer and demonstrates the following:

- Navigating in the Viewer window
- Editing and saving output
- Displaying output as simple text

This tutorial uses the file *Employee data.sav*, described in previous chapters. If you need help opening the file, see Chapter 4.

## Creating Output

When you run a procedure, the results are displayed in a window called the Viewer. The Frequencies and Crosstabs output produced in this section will be used to illustrate several features of the Viewer.

❶ To obtain a frequencies analysis, from the menus choose:

Analyze
  Descriptive Statistics
    Frequencies...

❷ Move *Employment Category* to the Variable(s) list.

❸ Click Charts and select Bar charts.

The dialog boxes are shown in Figure 5.1.

**Figure 5.1    Frequencies dialog boxes**

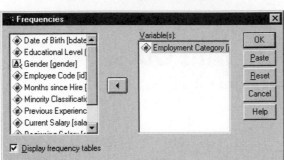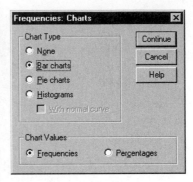

④ Click Continue and then OK.

⑤ To obtain a crosstabulation, from the menus choose:

Analyze
  Descriptive Statistics
    Crosstabs...

⑥ Move *Employment Category* to the Row(s) list.

⑦ Move *Gender* to the Column(s) list.

⑧ Move *Minority Classification* to the Layer list.

The dialog box should appear as shown in Figure 5.2.

**Figure 5.2    Crosstabs dialog box**

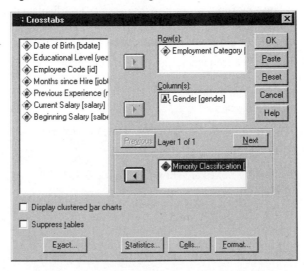

**⑨** Click OK.

The results are displayed in the Viewer window, as shown in Figure 5.3.

**Figure 5.3    Crosstabulation displayed in Viewer window**

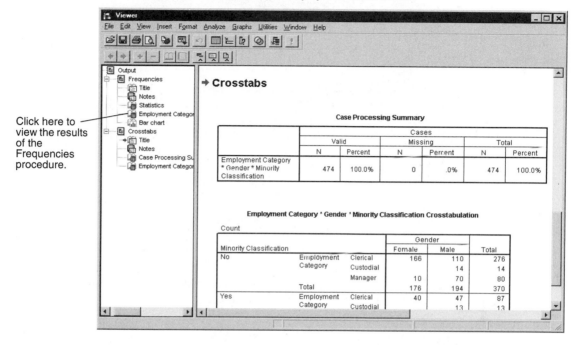

## Navigating in the Viewer Window

In the Viewer window, you can easily navigate to whichever part of the output you want to see.

To examine your output:

**①** Click anywhere in the Viewer to make it the active window. (You might also want to maximize the Viewer so that more of the output is visible.)

**②** Click Employment Category under Frequencies in the outline pane to move to the output from the Frequencies procedure. Notice that a red arrow appears next to the Frequencies table in the contents pane and next to its title in the outline pane (see Figure 5.4).

**Figure 5.4    Selected table in the Viewer window**

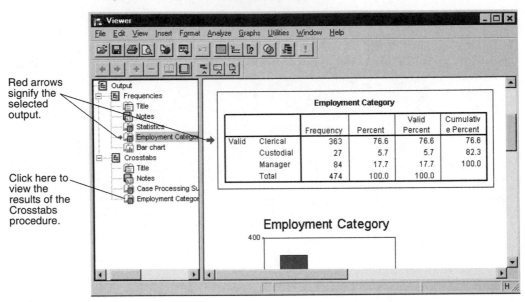

Red arrows signify the selected output.

Click here to view the results of the Crosstabs procedure.

**3** Move to the output from the Crosstabs procedure by clicking on its title in the outline pane. Alternatively, you can use the scroll bar to move to it.

## Modifying Pivot Tables

The Crosstabs and Frequencies procedures (and most other statistical procedures) produce output in the form of pivot tables. With pivot tables, you can:

- Transpose rows and columns.
- Move rows and columns.
- Create multidimensional layers.

To pivot a table or make other modifications:

**1** Double-click the Crosstabs table to activate it.

**2** From the menus choose:

Pivot
  Pivoting Trays

**Figure 5.5    Activated pivot table with pivoting trays**

Pivoting trays

Pivot icon for minority

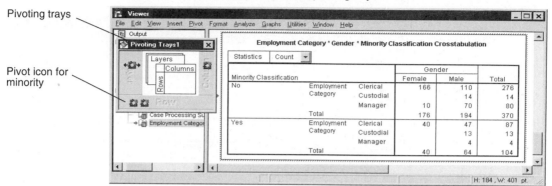

❸ Click on any pivot icon in the pivoting trays to identify the table dimension represented by the icon. The selected dimension appears shaded in the pivot table.

❹ Click and drag the pivot icon for *Minority Classification* from the Row dimension to the Layer dimension. This means that instead of having all of the information in one table, there are two tables—one on top of the other.

The table now contains multiple layers, with each category of *Minority Classification* contained in a separate layer; so each layer displays a crosstabulation of *Gender* and *Employment Category* for a different category of *Minority Classification*.

❺ Click the arrows on the pivot icon for *Minority Classification* to change the displayed layer.

Alternatively, you can select a new layer from the Minority Classification dropdown list.

**Figure 5.6    Changing display order in a pivot table**

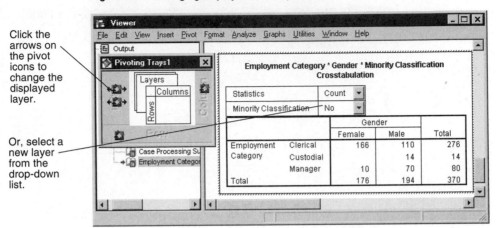

Click the arrows on the pivot icons to change the displayed layer.

Or, select a new layer from the drop-down list.

You can also change the display order of rows or columns in a pivot table.

**6** Click and drag the column label *Male* on top of the column label *Female*.

**7** Choose Swap from the pop-up menu.

The positions of the two columns are now switched.

## Customizing Output with Scripts

You are provided with a scripting facility that enables you to automate many tasks, including modifying pivot tables. You can create your own scripts or use and modify the scripts that are included with the software.

*Note*: Scripting is not available in the Student Version.

**1** Click outside any tables and then click the crosstabulation pivot table to select it. (Don't double-click the table; you only want to select it, not to activate it.)

**2** From the menus choose:

Utilities
  Run Script...

**3** From the *Scripts* directory, select *Make totals bold.sbs*.

**Figure 5.7    Using scripts to customize output**

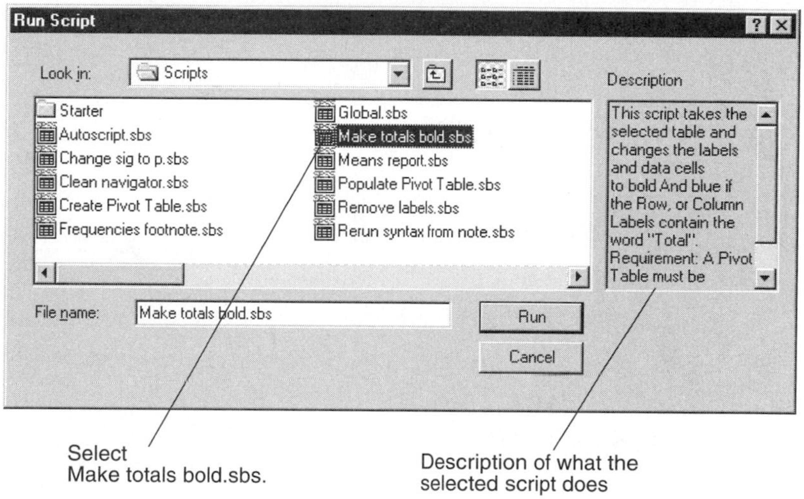

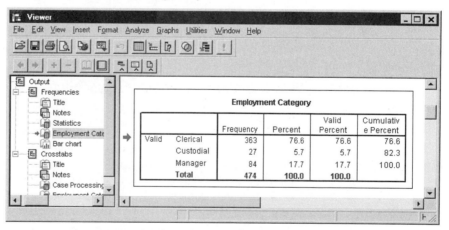

Select
Make totals bold.sbs.

Description of what the
selected script does

❹ Click Run to run the script.

**Figure 5.8    Bold totals using a script**

| Employment Category | | | | | |
|---|---|---|---|---|---|
| | | Frequency | Percent | Valid Percent | Cumulative Percent |
| Valid | Clerical | 363 | 76.6 | 76.6 | 76.6 |
| | Custodial | 27 | 5.7 | 5.7 | 82.3 |
| | Manager | 84 | 17.7 | 17.7 | 100.0 |
| | **Total** | **474** | **100.0** | **100.0** | |

The totals are now displayed in bold (and blue).

### Autoscripts

An autoscript file is a collection of script subroutines that run automatically each time you run procedures that create certain types of output objects. To activate the autoscript file and autoscript subroutines:

❶ From the menus choose:

Edit
  Options...

❷ Click the Scripts tab.

❸ Select Enable Autoscripting.

❹ Select the autoscript subroutines that you want to enable.

❺ You can also specify a different autoscript file or global procedure file.

## Saving Output

To save a Viewer document:

❶ From the Viewer menus choose:

File
  Save

❷ Type a name for the document and click Save.

To save output in external formats (for example, HTML or text), use Export on the File menu.

## Pasting Viewer Output into Another Application

You can paste your output into another Windows application, such as a word-processing program.

- To copy and paste a single output table or chart, select the item (click it once to select it) and choose Copy from the Edit menu. In the target application, choose Paste from the Edit menu. The item is pasted as a metafile, a bitmap, or unformatted text depending on the other application. Use Paste Special in the other application to control the pasted format.

- To copy and paste multiple output items, select the items (Shift-click or Ctrl-click to select multiple items), and choose Copy objects from the Edit menu. In the target application, choose Paste from the Edit menu.

- To paste pivot tables as text into another application, choose Paste Special from the Edit menu in the target application, and then select Unformatted text. When pasting into Word, pivot tables can be rendered as editable tables in rich text format (RTF).

## Displaying Output as Simple Text in the Draft Viewer

The Draft Viewer allows you to view a "draft" version of your output. You can get tables formatted in simple text (instead of interactive pivot tables) and charts in metafile format (instead of editable chart objects).

Text output in the Draft Viewer can be edited, charts can be resized, and both text output and charts can be pasted into other applications. However, charts cannot be edited, and the interactive features of pivot tables and charts are not available.

To produce draft output for the Frequencies procedure:

**1** From the menus choose:

File
  New
    Draft Output

This opens a new Draft Viewer window. All procedures you run will be displayed in this window until another window is designated.

**2** From the menus choose:

Analyze
  Descriptive Statistics
    Frequencies...

**3** Move *Employment Category* to the Variable(s) list.

**4** Click Charts and select Bar charts.

**5** Click Continue and then OK.

The Frequency table is in simple text format, as shown in Figure 5.9. The bar chart is in metafile format.

**Figure 5.9    Frequency analysis in the Draft Viewer**

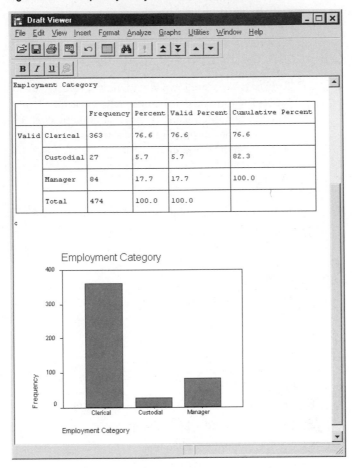

In the Draft Viewer, you can navigate between output tables from various procedures by using the scroll bars or the cursor. The Draft Viewer window has only one pane, the contents pane.

## Pasting Draft Output into Another Application

You can paste draft output into another application.

- To copy and paste a table, highlight the whole table and choose **Copy** from the Edit menu. In the target application, choose **Paste** from the Edit menu. The item is pasted as RTF or simple text, depending upon the application.

If you want to keep the spacing of the table, use a fixed-pitch font, such as Courier New.

- To copy and paste a chart, click the chart to select it and choose Copy from the Edit menu. In the target application, choose Paste from the Edit menu.

## What's Next?

At this point, you can exit or continue with the next tutorial. If you exit and you have changed the data file in any way, you will be asked whether you want to save the changes. Do *not* save changes to the *Employee data.sav* data file.

# 6 Tutorial: Creating and Modifying Interactive Bar Charts

This tutorial introduces the basics of creating interactive charts by using the Interactive submenu of the Graphs menu. It demonstrates the following:

- Creating an interactive bar chart that summarizes groups of cases
- Modifying the legend to create a clustered bar chart
- Displaying mean values within a bar chart
- Applying a ChartLook
- Pasting an interactive chart into another application

This tutorial uses the file *Employee data.sav*, described in previous chapters. If you need help opening the file, see Chapter 4. Standard (non-interactive) charts are discussed in Appendix A and Appendix B. If you want to edit a chart created by a statistical procedure such as Frequencies, follow the instructions for standard charts.

**Drag and drop.** For interactive charts, variables are moved in the dialog boxes using the drag-and-drop technique. (This is different from other dialog boxes in the system, in which a variable is moved by clicking an arrow button.)

# Creating the Chart

Figure 6.1 shows a simple bar chart that plots the number of cases within each employment category.

**Figure 6.1    Bar chart**

*A single categorical variable (Employment Category) is summarized. Each bar represents the number of cases for a category.*

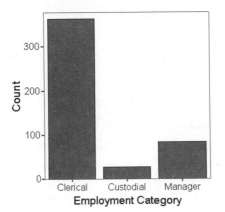

To create the chart shown in Figure 6.1:

❶ From the menus choose:

Graphs
  Interactive
    Bar...

This opens the Create Bar Chart dialog box, as shown in Figure 6.2.

❷ Click Reset to restore the default settings.

**Figure 6.2    Create Bar Chart dialog box**

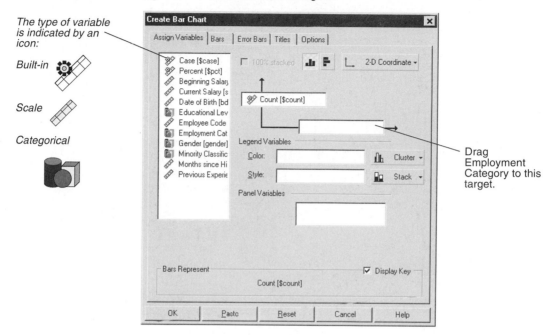

*The type of variable is indicated by an icon:*

*Built-in*

*Scale*

*Categorical*

Drag Employment Category to this target.

*Count* is assigned to the vertical axis by default.

Three types of variables are available in the variable list: built-in, scale, and categorical. A **built-in** data dimension creates a chart based on counts or percentages of cases found in your data. An example is *Count*, which produces a chart based on counts of the cases in each category.

A **scale** data dimension produces a chart in which a function of the variable is plotted (for example, the mean value). *Current Salary* is an example of a scale variable.

A **categorical** data dimension produces a chart with tick marks that indicate discrete values, with no values between the ticks. *Employment Category* is an example of a categorical variable. Its categories are *Clerical*, *Custodial*, and *Manager*.

❸ Click the categorical variable *Employment Category*, hold down the left mouse button, and drag the variable to the horizontal axis target.

*Warning*: Do not drag the scale variable *Employee Code* to the horizontal axis. Such an assignment will produce a chart with over 400 bars, completely filling the chart area.

❹ Click OK.

The chart is displayed in the Viewer, as shown in Figure 6.3.

**Figure 6.3    Bar chart in the Viewer**

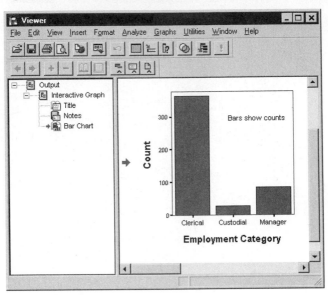

## Modifying the Legend

Suppose you want to see how genders are represented in the employee categories. You can modify the legend to produce a gender breakdown in the chart.

❶ Double-click the chart to activate it.

❷ Click the Assign Graph Variables tool    to open the Assign Graph Variables dialog box.

**Figure 6.4    Assign Graph Variables dialog box**

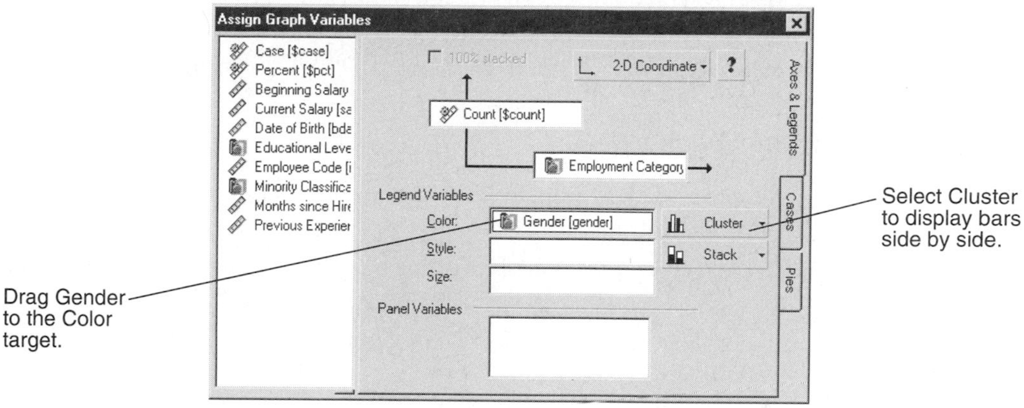

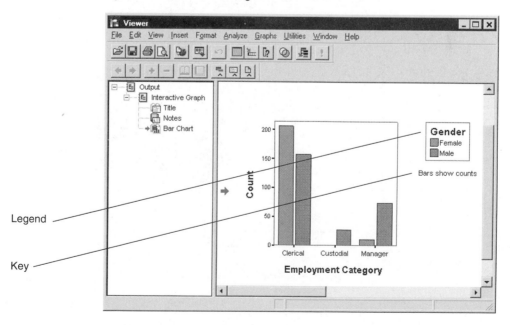

**❸** Drag *Gender* to the Color target under Legend Variables.

**❹** Select Cluster bars from the drop-down list.

The chart is displayed in the Viewer, as shown in Figure 6.5.

**Figure 6.5    Bar chart with legend in the Viewer**

Because *Gender* is a categorical variable, the bars are divided into two categories: male and female. The legend shows how the colors are assigned to each gender. You can see that in this data set, there are more females in clerical positions and more males in managerial positions.

## Displaying Mean Values

Suppose you now want to see what the mean current salaries are for each employment category.

**1** In the Assign Graph Variables dialog box, drag *Gender* back to the variable list.

**2** Drag *Current Salary* to the vertical axis and drop it on top of *Count*. In the dialog box, the variables switch places. *Count* automatically returns to the variable list.

The key now indicates that bars show means instead of counts, as shown in Figure 6.6.

**Figure 6.6    Bar chart showing mean current salary**

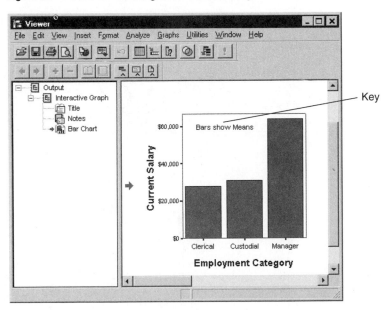

## Adding Error Bars

Often, you want to know the variability of the summary being represented. Error bars can be added to a chart representing mean values. To add error bars:

**1** Close the Assign Graph Variables dialog box.

**2** Click the Insert tool ![insert tool icon] on the toolbar.

**3** Select Error Bar.

The chart with error bars is displayed in the Viewer, as shown in Figure 6.7. A new key indicates that the error bars show the 95% confidence interval of the mean.

**Figure 6.7    Bar chart with error bars**

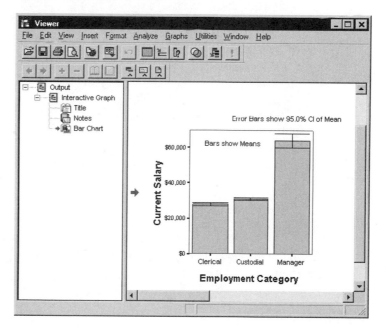

## Applying a ChartLook

You can customize the appearance of a chart by applying a ChartLook. Chart-Looks can be used to improve the appearance of charts for presentations and reports or to standardize features such as color and type size.

**1** In the Viewer, double-click the chart to activate it.

**2** From the menus choose:

Format
  ChartLooks...

This opens the ChartLook dialog box, as shown in Figure 6.8. It displays a list of ChartLooks that are stored in the *Looks* directory.

**Figure 6.8    ChartLook dialog box**

**3** Select Marina from the list of ChartLooks.

**4** Click Apply and then Close.

### Displaying Error Bars

The Marina ChartLook can be used for a dramatic color presentation. However, the lower part of each green error bar does not show up because it is the same color as its associated bar. To remedy this problem, you can change the color and style of the error bars.

**1** Double-click an error bar.

This opens the Error Bar dialog box, as shown in Figure 6.9.

**Figure 6.9    Error Bar dialog box**

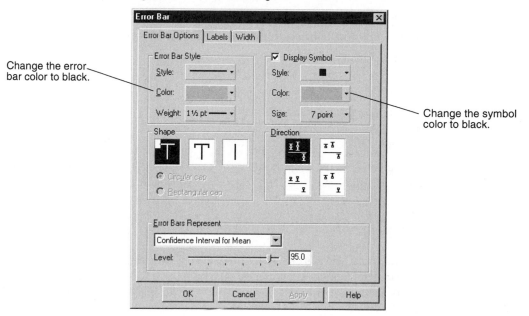

Change the error bar color to black.

Change the symbol color to black.

**2** Under Error Bar Style, click the Color drop-down list and select black.

**3** Under Display Symbol, click the Color drop-down list and select black.

**4** Click OK.

In general, you can modify a chart element by double-clicking on it and then making selections from a dialog box.

## Pasting a Chart into Another Application

You may want to paste your chart into another application and print the final document in black and white. First, a ChartLook that is good for black and white printing (such as Grayscale) should be selected.

**1** In the Viewer, double-click the chart to activate it.

**2** From the menus choose:

Format
  ChartLooks...

**3** Select Grayscale from the list of ChartLooks.

**4** Click Apply and then Close.

This applies a grayscale look, which prints well in black and white.

**⑤** Click in the Viewer outside the chart to deactivate the chart.

**⑥** Click once within the chart to select it.

**⑦** From the menus choose:

Edit
 Copy

**⑧** From the target application's menus choose:

Edit
 Paste

The chart is ready for printing in the other application. (You cannot edit the chart after it has been pasted to the other application.)

## What's Next?

At this point, you can choose to continue experimenting with the Graphs menu, continue with the next tutorial (in which you will learn how to create scatterplots), or exit the program. If you exit, do *not* save any changes to the *Employee data.sav* file.

# 7 Tutorial: Creating and Modifying Interactive Scatterplots

This tutorial introduces the basics of creating a chart from scratch and adding objects interactively. It demonstrates the following:

- Starting with a blank chart
- Creating an interactive scatterplot
- Labeling points in a scatterplot
- Adding a regression line to a scatterplot
- Adding adjustable mean prediction lines

This tutorial uses the file *Employee data.sav*, described in previous chapters. If you need help opening the file, see Chapter 4. Standard (non-interactive) charts are discussed in Appendix A and Appendix B.

**Drag and drop.** For interactive charts, variables are moved within the dialog boxes using the drag-and-drop technique. (This is different from other dialog boxes in the system, in which a variable is moved by clicking an arrow button.)

# Creating a Scatterplot

A scatterplot shows the relationship between two continuous variables, such as *Current Salary* and *Beginning Salary,* as shown in Figure 7.1.

**Figure 7.1    Scatterplot**

This tutorial starts with a chart that has a blank data region. The appropriate menus are in the Viewer.

❶ If the Viewer is not displayed, from the menus choose:

File
  New
    Output

This opens a new Viewer window.

❷ From the menus choose:

Insert
  Interactive 2-D Graph

This inserts a blank two-dimensional chart, as shown in Figure 7.2.

**Figure 7.2    Blank two-dimensional chart**

Click the Assign Graph Variables icon.

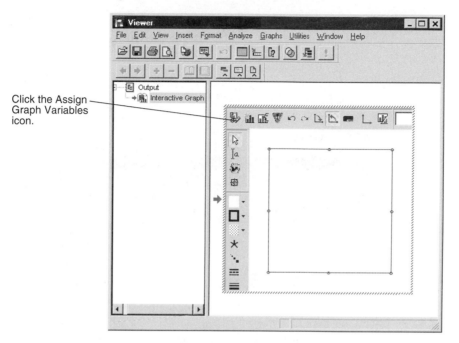

❸ Click the Assign Graph Variables icon  to open the Assign Graph Variables dialog box.

**Figure 7.3    Assign Graph Variables dialog box**

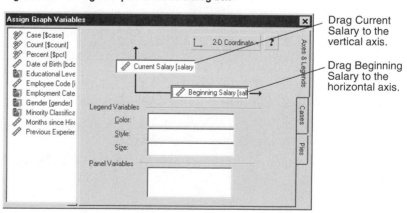

Drag Current Salary to the vertical axis.

Drag Beginning Salary to the horizontal axis.

④ Drag *Beginning Salary* from the variable list to the horizontal axis.

⑤ Drag *Current Salary* from the variable list to the vertical axis.

The chart is still blank because the type of chart has not been selected.

⑥ From the menus choose:

Insert
  Cloud

This creates a scatterplot, as shown in Figure 7.4.

**Figure 7.4    Scatterplot**

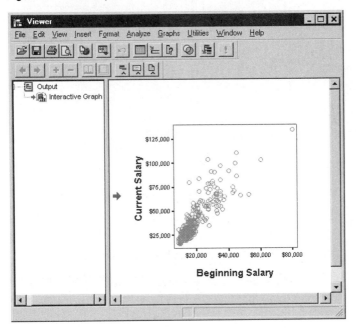

## Labeling Points in the Scatterplot

Suppose you want to label some or all of the individual points with the number of months of previous employment.

① In the Assign Graph Variables dialog box, select the Cases tab.

**Figure 7.5    Cases tab**

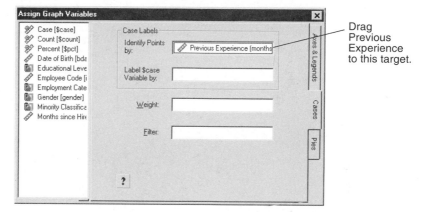

Drag
Previous
Experience
to this target.

❷ Drag *Previous Experience* from the variable list to the Identify Points target.

❸ Close the Assign Graph Variables dialog box.

❹ In the chart, while pressing the Ctrl key, click on three plot symbols near the high end of the vertical scale, as shown in Figure 7.6.

**Figure 7.6    Three selected cases**

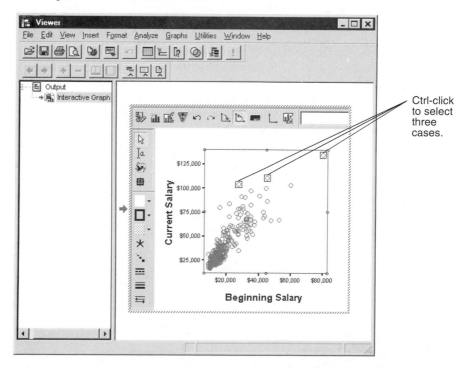

Ctrl-click
to select
three
cases.

⑤ Right-click on one of the selected cases.

⑥ From the context menu, choose Properties to open the Symbol Properties dialog box.

**Figure 7.7    Symbol Properties dialog box**

Select
Display Label.

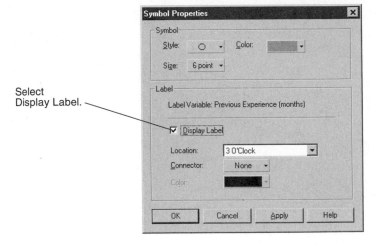

⑦ Select Display Label.

⑧ Click OK.

On the chart, the three selected cases are labeled with months of previous experience, as shown in Figure 7.8. The numbers shown suggest that further investigation might be interesting. However, this tutorial will go on to explain other graphical features in the next section.

In the Symbol Properties dialog box, you can also change the style, color, and size of the symbols on your chart.

**Figure 7.8    Labeled cases**

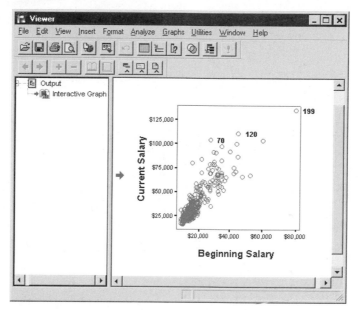

## Adding a Regression Line

The points in the scatterplot appear to fall roughly along a straight line. Several methods are available to fit a line to the points. A commonly used method of fitting a line is called **regression**.

❶ To draw a line that fits the distribution of points, from the menus choose:

Insert
  Fit Line
    Regression

This inserts a regression line into the scatterplot, as shown in Figure 7.9. Also displayed are labels that contain the equation of the line and a value for $R$-square, a statistic that indicates the goodness of fit of the line. $R$-square values can range from 0 to 1; the closer to 1, the better the fit.

**Figure 7.9    Regression line in the scatterplot**

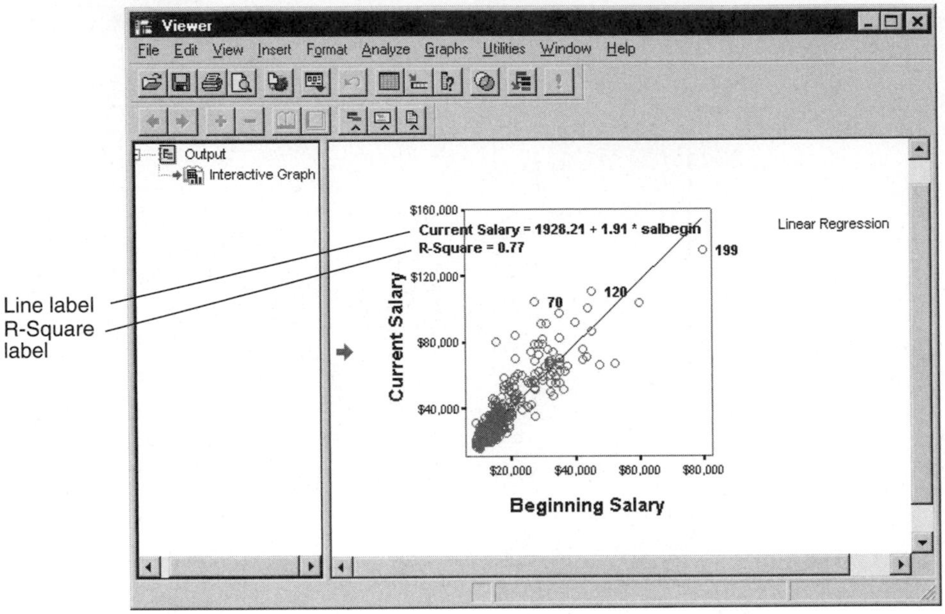

Some features of interactive charts can be dragged to new positions. Drag the labels to an area above the chart for better readability. You can also experiment with dragging the axis titles to new positions.

**Figure 7.10    Repositioned labels**

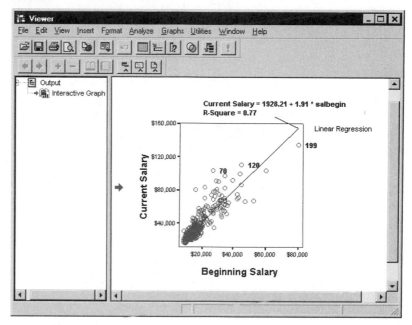

More information can be presented by showing the mean prediction interval, which consists of lines that indicate the boundaries of the area in which predicted values will fall (at a specified confidence level).

❷ Select the regression line by clicking on it once.

❸ From the menus choose:

Edit
  Regression Parameters...

This opens the Regression Parameters dialog box, as shown in Figure 7.11.

**Figure 7.11    Regression Parameters dialog box**

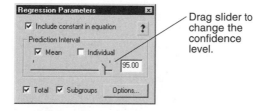

❹ Select Mean to add a mean prediction interval. Before closing the dialog box, you can drag the slider and watch the lines move as the confidence level of the mean prediction interval changes. The percentage value in the prediction interval key also reflects the changes made by moving the slider.

⑤ Click Options to change regression line, label, and key options.

This opens the Regression Options dialog box, as shown in Figure 7.12.

**Figure 7.12    Regression Options dialog box**

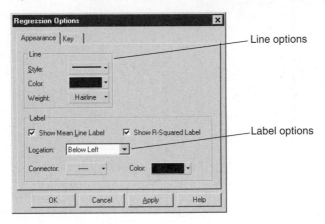

For a selected mean or regression fit line, you can change the style, color, weight, and label. For a regression fit line, you can also choose Show R-Squared Label. You can also change the location, title, and alignment of the regression line key by selecting the Key tab.

**Figure 7.13     Mean prediction interval**

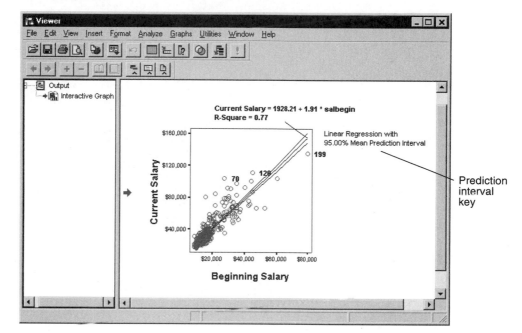

## What's Next?

At this point, you can continue experimenting with interactive charts, continue with the next tutorial, or exit the program. If you exit, do *not* save any changes to the *Employee data.sav* data file.

# Tutorial: 3-D Charts, Panels, and More Interactive Chart Features

The interactive graphics facility contains many features for customizing your charts. This tutorial demonstrates the following:

- Creating an interactive area chart
- Using tools to change colors and patterns
- Creating a panel for each category
- Using a third dimension to illustrate differences between categories
- Rotating a 3-D chart
- Editing chart components using the Chart Manager

This tutorial uses the file *Employee data.sav*, described in previous chapters. If you need help opening the file, see Chapter 4. Standard (non-interactive) charts are discussed in Appendix A and Appendix B.

**Drag and drop.** For interactive charts, variables are moved in the dialog boxes using the drag-and-drop technique. (This is different from other dialog boxes in the system, where a variable is moved by clicking an arrow button.)

## Creating an Area Chart

A simple area chart is like a line chart with the space below the line filled in. Area charts are helpful when there are too many data points to represent with bars. These data points form the upper limit of the area. The baseline of an area chart is always 0.

In Figure 8.1, the filled area represents the number of employees who have completed each level of education. The legend shows that females are represented by a dark color and males, by a light color. The educational differences between males and females are also illustrated.

**Figure 8.1    Area chart**

*The baseline of an area chart is always 0.*

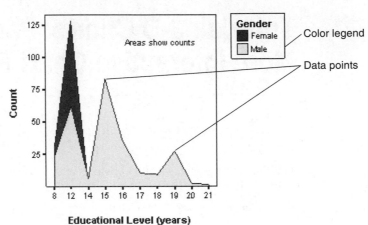

In Figure 8.1, you can see that most of the females in the data set have completed 12 years of education. Males, as the chart shows, have a greater spread in education levels. More than half have some level of college education, and a small number of males have completed graduate work.

As this 2-D area chart illustrates, it is difficult to see the complete area chart for females since it is clustered behind the chart for males. Later in this chapter, you will learn how to create both paneled and 3-D area charts. These types of charts will help you to see all aspects of your data and to determine which is the best view.

To create an area chart, from the menus choose:

Graphs
　Interactive
　　Area...

This opens the Create Area Chart dialog box.

❶ Click Reset to restore all of the default settings.

❷ Drag *Educational Level* to the horizontal axis. Also drag *Gender* to Legend Variables Color, as shown in Figure 8.2.

**Figure 8.2    Create Area Chart dialog box**

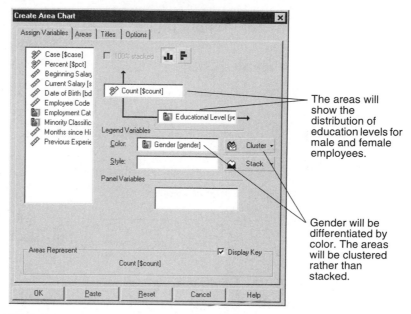

The areas will show the distribution of education levels for male and female employees.

Gender will be differentiated by color. The areas will be clustered rather than stacked.

❸  Click OK.

**Figure 8.3    Area chart of Education Level by Gender**

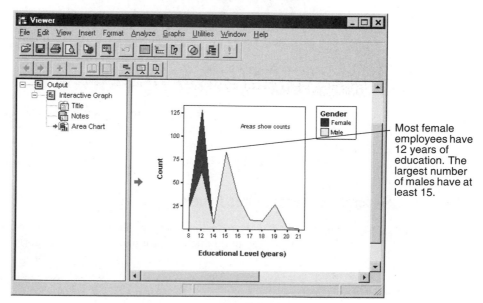

Most female employees have 12 years of education. The largest number of males have at least 15.

In Figure 8.3, the area charts are clustered. This means that one area chart is placed behind the other. To compare educational levels by gender more easily, you can stack the area charts.

## Creating a Stacked Chart

Another way to compare categories is by stacking the area charts.

❶ Double-click to activate the chart.

❷ Click the Assign Graph Variables tool 🖲 to open the Assign Graph Variables dialog box.

❸ From the Cluster drop-down list, choose Stack.

**Figure 8.4    Stacked area chart**

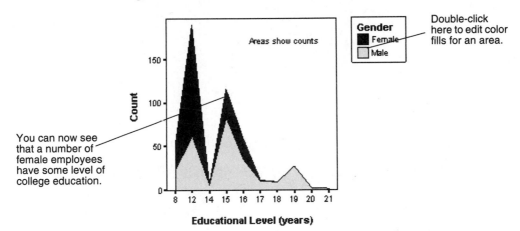

You can now see that a number of female employees have some level of college education.

Double-click here to edit color fills for an area.

In stacked charts, the top of the category for males forms the base of the category for females. Stacked charts emphasize the sum of the categories and the flow along the independent axis. However, in this type of chart, specific values of individual categories cannot be easily determined.

## Separating the Chart into Panels for Categories

Suppose you want to better compare the educational levels for males and females. One way to do this is to use panels for the categories of the variable *gender.*

❶ Click the Assign Graph Variables tool 🖲 to open the Assign Graph Variables dialog box.

❷ Drag *Gender* from the Legend list to the Panel Variables list, as shown in Figure 8.5.

**Figure 8.5    Assign Graph Variables dialog box**

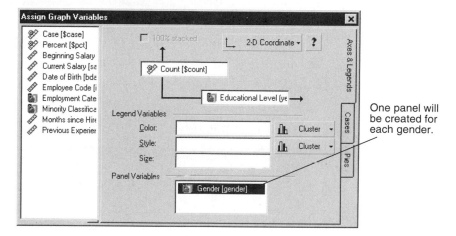

One panel will be created for each gender.

This produces a panel for each gender, as shown in Figure 8.6.

**Figure 8.6    Panels for male and female**

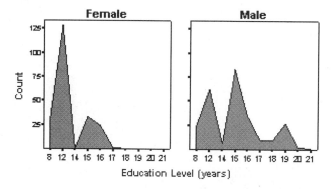

By looking at the *Female* panel, you can now see that there are at least 25 females with several years of college education. In 2-D clustered charts, you could not see this part of the data set because it was hidden behind the area for males. In these side-by-side panels, you can compare the gender differences more easily.

## Comparing Categories in Three Dimensions

Another way to compare categories is by adding a third dimension.

**1** In the Assign Graph Variables dialog box, select 3-D Coordinate from the drop-down list.

Notice that another axis target is added to the dialog box.

**2** Drag *Minority Classification* to the new axis.

**3** Drag *Gender* from the Panel Variables list to Legend Variable Color.

The 3-D area chart is shown in Figure 8.7, along with the 3-D tool palette.

**Figure 8.7    3-D area chart**

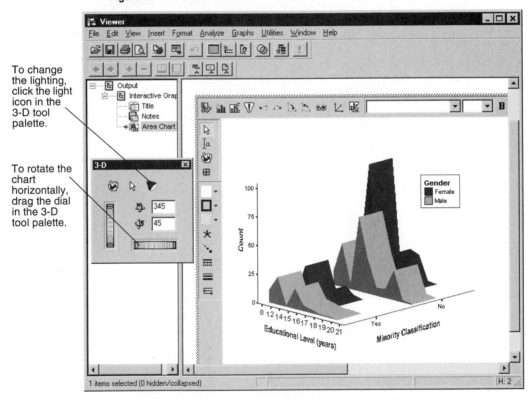

To change the lighting, click the light icon in the 3-D tool palette.

To rotate the chart horizontally, drag the dial in the 3-D tool palette.

This 3-D chart compares the differences in education by gender and minority status. You can see that nonminority males have the most education, while minority females have the least. The area charts here are clustered by minority classification.

Since it is difficult to see the nonminority female category, you can rotate the chart using the 3-D tools. With the mouse, drag the horizontal dial from right to left, to about 135 degrees. This shows you the number of nonminority females who have some college education.

## Changing the Attributes of Chart Components

Often you can access dialog boxes to change the properties of a chart component by double-clicking the element. Another way to access these dialog boxes is by using the Chart Manager.

**❶** Click the Chart Manager tool ![icon] from the toolbar of an activated map.

This displays the Chart Manager dialog box, as shown in Figure 8.8. The various components in the chart are listed under Chart Contents.

**Figure 8.8    Chart Manager dialog box**

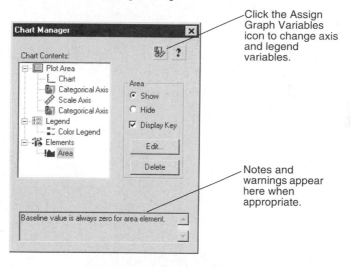

Click the Assign Graph Variables icon to change axis and legend variables.

Notes and warnings appear here when appropriate.

**❷** Drag the Chart Manager dialog box outside of the chart.

**❸** Select Chart and click Edit.

This displays the Data Region dialog box.

**Figure 8.9    Data Region dialog box**

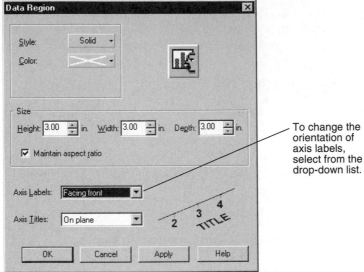

④ Near the bottom of the dialog box, from the Axis Labels drop-down list choose
Facing front and click OK.

**Figure 8.10    Rotated 3-D area chart**

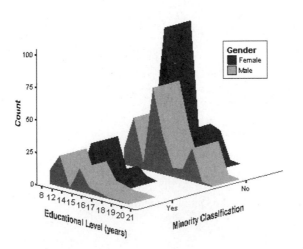

The axis labels are now facing the front of the chart. You can experiment with
changing other attributes of various chart components—perhaps change the

light source (from the 3-D tool palette), stack the charts, or change the axis range for *Educational Level* (double-click the axis).

## Changing Colors and Patterns with Tools

Many tools are available to change the appearance of objects in the chart. To change the fill color of the areas:

❶ In the activated chart, double-click a color box in the legend. This opens the Color Legend dialog box.

❷ Select a category, such as Female, from the list.

❸ Select a color from the palette and click OK to apply.

**Figure 8.11    Color Legend dialog box**

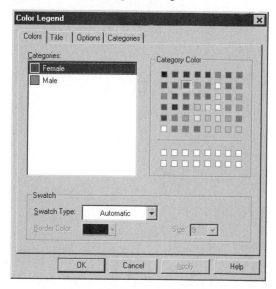

Other tools are available to change the border color and the style or pattern of filled objects. You can also use tools to change the symbol style, symbol size, line style, line size, and connector style.

# What's Next?

At this point, you can continue experimenting with charts, continue with the next tutorial (in which you will learn how to modify data values), or exit the program. If you exit, do *not* save any changes to the *Employee data.sav* file.

# 9 Tutorial: Modifying Data Values

There are numerous facilities for modifying data values and creating new variables based on transformations of existing variables. This tutorial introduces the use of the Transform menu and demonstrates the use of the Recode option to recode a continuous variable into distinct categories.

## Recoding Data Values

One of the most useful data transformations is accomplished with the Recode facility, which is used to combine categories of a variable.

For example, you can't use actual salaries in a crosstabulation to show the relationship between salary and gender because very few people are likely to have the same salary. The number of distinct "categories" for salary would likely be almost as large as the number of cases in your data file. You could, however, create a new variable that combines salary ranges into a small number of categories, such as less than $25,000, $25,000 to $49,999, and $50,000 or more.

**1** Open the file *Employee data.sav*, which is described in previous chapters. If you need help opening the file, see Chapter 4.

**2** From the menus choose:

Transform
  Recode
    Into Different Variables...

This opens the Recode into Different Variables dialog box.

**3** Select *Current Salary* on the variable list and click the arrow button to move it to the Numeric Variable –> Output Variable list, as shown in Figure 9.1.

**Figure 9.1    Recode into Different Variables dialog box**

*To recode a string variable into consecutive integer values, you can use the Automatic Recode option on the Transform menu.*

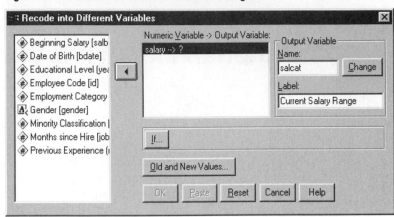

**④** In the Output Variable group, type **salcat** into the Name text box.

**⑤** In the Output Variable group, type **Current Salary Range** into the Label text box.

**⑥** Click Change.

The original variable name and the new variable name are displayed together on the Numeric Variable –> Output Variable list.

**⑦** Click Old and New Values.

This opens the Old and New Values dialog box, as shown in Figure 9.2.

**Figure 9.2    Old and New Values dialog box**

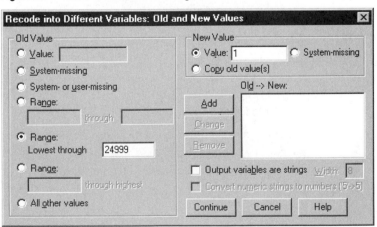

⑧ In the Old Value group, select Range: Lowest through.

⑨ Type **24999** into the Lowest Through text box.

⑩ In the New Value group, select Value.

⑪ Type **1** into the Value text box.

⑫ Click Add.

Lowest thru 24999 –> 1 is displayed on the Old –> New list (see Figure 9.3). This means that all salaries below $25,000 will be combined into a single category coded 1 for the new variable, *Current Salary Range*.

⑬ In the Old Value group, select the first Range bullet.

⑭ Type **25000** into the first Range text box.

⑮ Type **49999** into the second Range text box.

⑯ In the New Value group, selcct Value, type **2** into the text box, and then click Add.

⑰ In the Old Value group, select Range: through highest and type **50000** into the text box.

⑱ In the New Value group, select Value, type **3** into the text box, and then click Add.

The Old and New Values dialog box should now look like Figure 9.3.

**Figure 9.3    Completed Old and New Values dialog box**

*Any unspecified old values will be set to system-missing for the new variable. If you don't want to recode all values, select All other values and select Copy old value(s) to retain values not covered by the recoding scheme.*

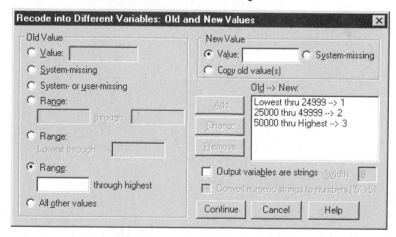

**19** Click Continue in the Old and New Values dialog box, and then click OK in the main Recode into Different Variables dialog box.

*If values for the new variable are not calculated after you click OK, choose Run Pending Transformations from the Transform menu.*

The new variable *Current Salary Range* is added to the data file and is the last column displayed in the Data Editor window. You can add descriptive value labels for the numeric category codes by switching to Variable View and adding labels in the *Value* column for the selected variable (see Chapter 3 for more information about defining variables).

*Note*: If values are not calculated for the new variable after you click OK, choose Run Pending Transformations from the Transform menu. (If you want to always run your transformations immediately, from the Edit menu, choose Options. Select the Data tab and be sure that the option Calculate values immediately is selected in the Transformation and Merge Options group.)

## What's Next?

At this point, you can exit the program or continue with the next tutorial. If you exit, and you have changed the data file in any way, you will be asked whether you want to save the changes. Do *not* save changes to the data file *Employee data.sav*.

*Note*: If you want to save the data file with the new variable created in this tutorial, you should use the Save As option on the File menu and give the file a new name.

# 10 Tutorial: Working with Syntax

This tutorial introduces the use of command syntax, an alternative way to run procedures. Using syntax also allows you to save the exact specifications used during a session. This tutorial demonstrates the following:

- Pasting syntax from a dialog box
- Typing syntax into a syntax window
- Editing syntax

*Note*: Syntax is not available in the Student Version.

## Pasting Syntax

The easiest way to construct a useful command is to paste the syntax from a dialog box. In this example, command syntax will be used to run the Frequencies procedure. The results are similar to those shown in Chapter 1.

**1** Open the file *Employee data.sav*, which is described in previous chapters. If you need help opening the file, see Chapter 4.

**2** From the menus choose:

Analyze
  Descriptive Statistics
    Frequencies...

This opens the Frequencies dialog box.

**3** Select *Employee Category* and move it to the Variable(s) list.

**4** Click Charts.

**5** In the Charts dialog box, select Bar charts, and in the Chart Values group, select Percentages. Then click Continue.

The Frequencies dialog box is displayed, as shown in Figure 10.1.

**Figure 10.1    Frequencies dialog box**

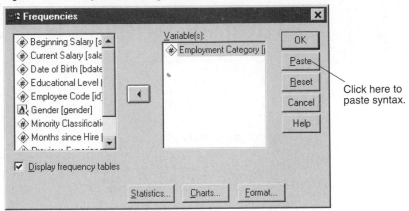

Click here to paste syntax.

**6** Click Paste (instead of OK).

This opens a syntax window and pastes the FREQUENCIES command into it, as shown in Figure 10.2.

**Figure 10.2    Syntax window**

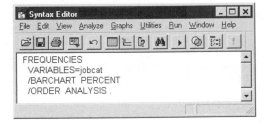

*To run several commands, highlight the commands and click*

**7** To run the command, make sure the cursor is within the command, and click the Run syntax tool   .

The results are the same as if you had clicked OK in the Frequencies dialog box.

# Editing Syntax

In the syntax window, you can edit the syntax. For example, you could change the subcommand /BARCHART to display frequencies instead of percentages, as shown in Figure 10.3. (A subcommand is indicated by a slash.)

**Figure 10.3    Modified syntax**

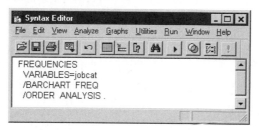

To find out what subcommands and keywords are available for the current command, click the Syntax Help tool. Complete syntax for the FREQUENCIES command is shown in Figure 10.4.

**Figure 10.4    FREQUENCIES syntax**

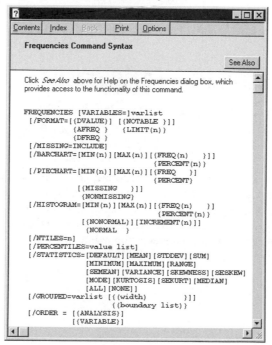

If the cursor is not in a command, clicking the Syntax Help tool displays an alphabetical list of commands. You can click the one you want.

## Typing Syntax

You can type syntax into a syntax window that is already open, or you can open a new syntax window by choosing:

File
  New
    Syntax

## Saving Syntax

To save a syntax file, from the menus choose:

File
  Save

*or*

File
  Save As...

This opens a standard dialog box for saving files.

## Opening and Running a Syntax File

To open a saved syntax file, from the menus choose:

File
  Open
    Syntax

Select a syntax file and click Open (if no syntax files are displayed, make sure Syntax (*.sps) is selected in the Files of Type drop-down list). Then run the commands by using the Run syntax tool, as described above. If the commands apply to a specific data file, the data file must be opened before running the commands, or you must include a command that opens the data file. You can paste this type of command from the dialog boxes that open data files.

## Additional Information

In the Help system, most procedures have a topic that discusses additional features available with the command language. For more information about how to use syntax, you can search the Help system for Syntax. You can also consult the *SPSS Syntax Reference Guide* that comes with SPSS for Windows.

## What's Next?

At this point, you can exit the program. When you exit and you have changed the data file in any way, you will be asked whether you want to save the changes. Do *not* save changes to the data file *Employee data.sav.*

The next chapter describes data files in different formats.

# 11 Data Files

The Data Editor is designed to handle a wide variety of formats, including:

- Spreadsheet files created with Lotus 1-2-3 and Excel
- Database files created with dBASE and various SQL formats
- Tab-delimited and other types of ASCII text files
- SPSS data files created on other operating systems
- SYSTAT data files

## Creating a New Data File

If your data are not already in computer files, you can use the Data Editor to enter the data and create a data file. The Data Editor is a simple, efficient spreadsheet-like facility that opens automatically when you start a session. For information about the Data Editor, see Chapter 3.

## Opening a Data File

To open a data file, from the menus in the Data Editor window choose:

File
  Open
    Data...

This opens the Open File dialog box, as shown in Figure 11.1.

**Figure 11.1    Open File dialog box**

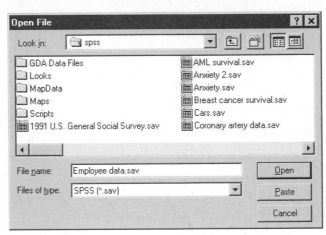

*If the extension of your data file is different from the default extension for the file type, select the file type from the File of Type drop-down list or type an asterisk (\*) followed by the file extension in the File Name field.*

## Specifying File Type

By default, a list of data files saved in SPSS format (*.sav*) is displayed in the dialog. To display a list of files in other formats, select the file format from the drop-down list of file types.

## Reading Variable Names

For Lotus, Excel, SYLK, and tab-delimited files, you can read variable names from the file. The values in the first row of the file (or cell range) are used as variable names. If variable names exceed eight characters, they are truncated. If they are not unique, they are modified.

## Reading a Range of Cells

For Lotus, Excel, and SYLK files, you can specify a range of cells to read.

- For Lotus files, specify the beginning column letter and row number, two periods, and the ending column letter and row number (for example, A1..K14).
- For Excel files, specify the beginning column letter and row number, a colon, and the ending column letter and row number (for example, A1:K14).

- For SYLK files and Excel files saved in R1C1 display format, specify the beginning and ending cells of the range separated by a colon (for example, R1C1:R14C11).

If you have defined a name for a range of cells in the spreadsheet file, you can enter the name in the Range text box.

## How the Data Editor Reads Spreadsheet Data

An SPSS data file is rectangular. The boundaries (or dimensions) of the data file are determined by the number of cases (rows) and variables (columns). There are no "empty" cells within the boundaries of the data file. All cells have a value, even if that value is "blank." The following general rules apply to reading spreadsheet data:

*If your spreadsheet is organized with cases in columns and variables in rows, use the Transpose option on the Data menu to put your data in the correct order after you read the data into the Data Editor.*

- Rows are considered cases, and columns are considered variables.

- The number of variables is determined by the last column with any non-blank cells or the total number of nonblank cells in the row containing variable names. If you read variable names, any columns with a blank cell for the variable name are not included in the data file.

- The number of cases is determined by the last row with any nonblank cells within the column boundaries defined by the number of variables (unless you read a range of cells).

- The data type and width for each variable are determined by the column width and data type of the first data cell in the column. Values of other types are converted to the system-missing value. If the first data cell in the column is blank, the global default data type for the spreadsheet (usually numeric) is used.

- For numeric variables, blank cells are converted to the system-missing value, indicated by a period.

- For string variables, a blank is a valid string value, and blank cells are treated as valid string values.

- If you do not read variable names from the spreadsheet, the column letters (*A*, *B*, *C*, etc.) are used as variable names for Excel and Lotus files. For SYLK files and Excel files saved in R1C1 display format, variable names use the column number preceded by the letter *C* for variable names (*C1*, *C2*, *C3*, etc.).

Figure 11.2 shows how the Data Editor reads a spreadsheet file that contains variable names, and Figure 11.3 shows how the Data Editor reads an Excel spreadsheet file that has no variable names.

**Figure 11.2    Reading spreadsheet data with variable names**

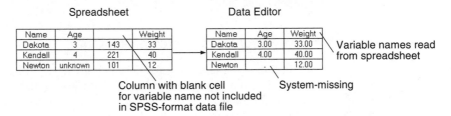

**Figure 11.3    Reading Excel spreadsheet file without variable names**

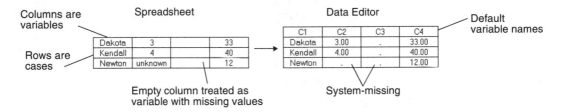

## How the Data Editor Reads dBASE Files

Database files are logically very similar to SPSS-format data files. The following general rules apply to dBASE files:

- Field names are automatically translated to variable names.

- Field names should comply with variable naming conventions for SPSS format. Field names longer than eight characters are truncated. If the first eight characters of the field name do not produce a unique name, the field is dropped.

- Colons used in dBASE field names are translated to underscores.

- Records marked for deletion but not actually purged are included. The software creates a new string variable, *D_R*, which contains an asterisk for cases marked for deletion.

## How the Data Editor Reads Tab-Delimited Files

The following general rules apply to reading tab-delimited files:

- Values can be either numeric or string. Any value that contains non-numeric characters is considered a string value. (Formats such as Dollar and Date are not recognized and are read as string values.)

- The data type and width for each variable are determined by the type and width of the first data value in the column. Values of other types are converted to the system-missing value.

- For numeric variables, the assigned width is eight digits or the number of digits in the first data value, whichever is greater. Values that exceed the defined width are rounded for display. The entire value is stored internally.

- For string variables, values that exceed the defined width are truncated.

- If you do not read variable names from the file, default names will be assigned, such as *var1*, *var2*, *var3*, etc.

## How the Data Editor Reads Data Files Using ODBC

You can read data from any database format for which you have an ODBC driver. Using the Database Capture Wizard, you can easily retrieve data from a variety of sources, such as Excel or Access, by using the corresponding ODBC driver. The Database Capture Wizard, shown in Figure 11.4, guides you through this process.

To open the Database Capture Wizard, from the menus choose:

File
  Open Database
    New Query...

**Figure 11.4    Database Capture Wizard**

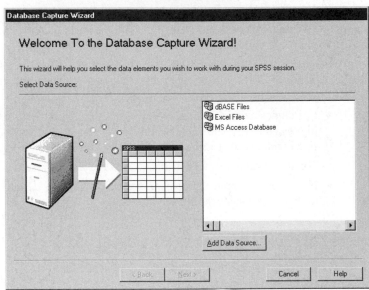

*In six steps, the Database Capture Wizard will help you select your data source and specify relationships between tables.*

## Reading Text Files

The Text Import Wizard will guide you through the process of reading text data into the Data Editor. You will have to answer questions about the type and arrangement of your data, number of cases you want to import, and missing values. The Text Import Wizard can read text data files formatted in a variety of ways.

- Tab-delimited files
- Space-delimited files
- Comma-delimited files
- Fixed-field format files

To read text data files, from the menus choose:

File
  Read Text Data

1. Select the text file in the Open dialog box.

2. Follow the steps in the Text Import Wizard to define how to read the data file.

3. Click the Help button in the Text Import Wizard for more detailed information on reading text data files.

Figure 11.5    Text Import Wizard Step 1

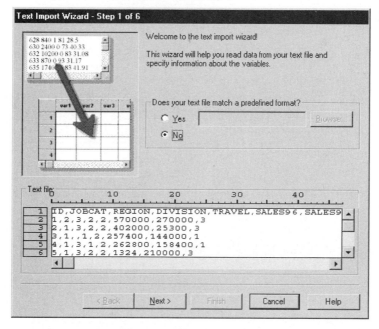

*When you have followed all the steps, click Finish to view the data in the Data Editor.*

*The text file is displayed in a preview window. In Step 1, you can apply a predefined format to your data. Click Next to continue using the Text Wizard.*

## Saving a Data File

You can save data files in any of the following formats:

- SPSS
- SPSS/PC+
- SPSS portable format (for use on other operating systems)
- Lotus 1-2-3

- Excel
- SYLK (symbolic link)
- dBASE
- Tab-delimited ASCII text
- Fixed-format ASCII text

To save a new data file:

1. Make the Data Editor the active window (by clicking anywhere in the Data Editor).

2. From the menus choose:

   File
     Save As...

This opens the Save Data As dialog box, as shown in Figure 11.6.

**Figure 11.6    Save Data As dialog box**

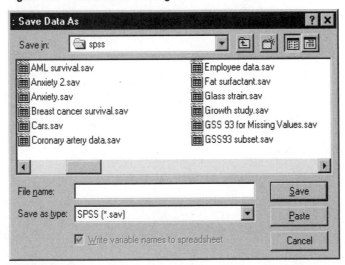

## Specifying File Type

Before you can save a data file, you need to determine what type of file it is. Regardless of the file extension, you must select the appropriate file type from the drop-down list. You cannot specify a different file type simply by changing the extension of the wildcard search in the File Name text box.

## Closing a Data File

Since only one data file can be open at a time, the Data Editor automatically closes the working data file before opening another one. If there have been any changes to the data file since it was last saved, you want to save the changes before it closes the file and opens the next one.

# 12 Calculating New Data Values

In an ideal situation, your raw data are perfectly suitable for the type of analysis you want to perform. Unfortunately, this is rarely the case. Preliminary analysis may reveal inconvenient coding schemes or coding errors, or data transformations may be required in order to coax out the true relationship between variables.

Using this software, you can perform data transformations ranging from simple tasks, such as collapsing categories for analysis, to creating new variables based on complex equations and conditional statements.

## Recoding Values

You can modify data values by recoding them. This is particularly useful for combining categories. You can recode the values within existing variables, or you can create new variables based on the recoded values of existing variables. For more information about recoding, see Chapter 9.

# Computing Values

To compute values for a variable based on numeric transformations of other variables, open a data file such as *Employee data.sav*. From the menus choose:

Transform
  Compute...

This opens the Compute Variable dialog box, as shown in Figure 12.1.

**Figure 12.1    Compute Variable dialog box**

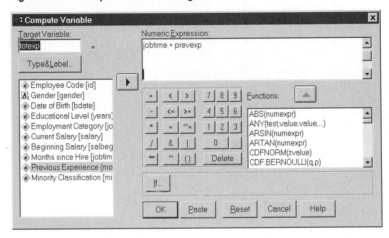

To compute a variable:

1. Enter a target variable name. If you enter an existing variable name, the computed values replace the original values.

2. Enter a numeric expression that will produce the desired computed value. If the computed value is based on the values of existing variables, select the variable names from the variable list and use the arrow button to move them into the Numeric Expression box.

For example, in Figure 12.1, the new variable *totexp* will be computed as the sum of variables *jobtime* and *prevexp*.

## Calculator Pad

The calculator pad contains numbers, arithmetic operators, relational operators, and logical operators (see Table 12.1). You can use it like a calculator (using the mouse to point and click on keys) or simply as a reference for the correct symbols to use for various operators.

**Table 12.1    Calculator pad operators**

| Arithmetic Operators | Relational Operators | Logical Operators |
|---|---|---|
| + Addition | < Less than | & And. Both relations must be true. |
| − Subtraction | > Greater than | \| Or. Either relation can be true. |
| * Multiplication | <= Less than or equal to | ~ Not. Reverses the true/false out- |
| / Division | >= Greater than or equal to | come of the expression. |
| ** Exponentiation | = Equal to | |
| ( ) Order of operations | ~= Not equal to | |

### Arithmetic Operators

Since fairly complex expressions are possible, it is important to keep in mind the order in which operations are performed. Functions are evaluated first, followed by exponentiation, then multiplication and division, and, finally, addition and subtraction. You can control the order of operations by enclosing in parentheses the operation you want to be executed first. You can use the ( ) key on the calculator pad to enclose a highlighted portion of the expression in parentheses.

### Relational Operators

A **relation** is a logical expression that compares two values using a relational operator. They are primarily used in conditional transformations (see "Relational and Logical Operators in Conditional Expressions" on p. 115).

### Logical Operators

You can use logical operators to join two relations or reverse the true/false outcome of a conditional expression. They are primarily used in conditional transformations (see "Relational and Logical Operators in Conditional Expressions" on p. 115).

## Functions

The function list contains over 70 built-in functions, including:

- Arithmetic functions
- Statistical functions
- Distribution functions
- Logical functions
- Date and time aggregation and extraction functions
- Missing-value functions
- Cross-case functions
- String functions

For information on specific functions, click your right mouse button on the function you want to know about or click Help in the Compute Variable dialog box.

### Pasting and Editing Functions

**Pasting a function into an expression**. To paste a function into an expression:

1. Position the cursor in the expression at the point where you want the function to appear.

2. Double-click on the function in the Functions list (or select the function and click the ▲ pushbutton).

The function is inserted into the expression. If you highlight part of the expression and then insert the function, the highlighted portion of the expression is used as the first argument in the function.

**Editing a function in an expression**. The function is not complete until you enter the arguments, represented by question marks in the pasted function. The number of question marks indicates the minimum number of arguments required to complete the function. To edit a function:

1. Highlight the question mark(s) in the pasted function.

2. Enter the arguments. If the arguments are variable names, you can paste them from the variable list.

## Conditional Expressions

You can use conditional expressions (also called logical expressions) to apply transformations to selected subsets of cases. A **conditional expression** returns a value of true, false, or missing for each case. If the result of a conditional expression is true, the transformation is applied to that case. If the result is false or missing, the transformation is not applied to the case.

To specify a conditional expression, click If in the Compute Variable dialog box. This opens the If Cases dialog box, as shown in Figure 12.2.

**Figure 12.2    If Cases dialog box**

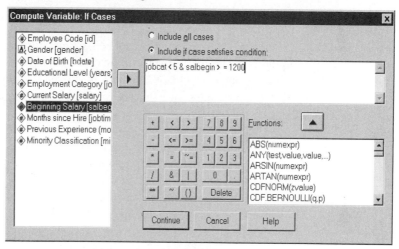

To specify a conditional expression:

1. Select Include if case satisfies condition.

2. Enter the conditional expression.

### Relational and Logical Operators in Conditional Expressions

Most conditional expressions contain at least one relational operator, as in

**age>=21**

*or*

**salary*3<100000**

In the first example, only cases with a value of 21 or greater for *age* are selected. In the second example, *salary* multiplied by 3 must be less than 100,000 for a case to be selected.

You can also link two or more conditional expressions using logical operators, as in

**age>=21 | jobcat=1**

*or*

**salary*3<100000 & jobcat~=5**

In the first example, cases that meet either the *age* condition or the *jobcat* condition are selected. In the second example, both the *salary* and *jobcat* conditions must be met for a case to be selected.

## Rules for Expressions

Items selected from the calculator pad, function list, and variable list are pasted in the correct format. If you type an expression in the text box or edit part of it (such as an argument to a function), remember the following simple rules:

- String variable values must be enclosed in apostrophes or quotation marks, as in **NAME='Fred'**. If the string value includes an apostrophe, enclose the string in quotation marks.
- The argument list for a function must be enclosed in parentheses. You can insert a space between the argument name and the parentheses, but none is required.
- Multiple arguments in a function must be separated by commas. You can insert spaces between arguments, but none is required.
- Each relation in a complex expression must be complete by itself. For example, **age>=18 & age<35** is correct, while **age>=18 & <35** generates an error.
- A period (.) is the only valid decimal indicator in expressions, regardless of your Windows International settings.

# Additional Data Transformations

The following additional data transformations are also available on the Transform menu:

- **Count**. Counts occurrences of the same value(s) across a list of variables within each case.
- **Rank Cases**. Computes ranks and normal and Savage scores, and classifies cases into groups based on percentile values.
- **Automatic Recode**. Recodes string and numeric variables into consecutive integers. This is useful for procedures that require integer data.

- **Create Time Series**. Creates new time series variables based on functions of existing time series variables. (Any variable measured regularly over a period of time is a time series variable.)
- **Replace Missing Values**. Replaces missing values in time series data with estimates computed with one of several methods.

# 13

# Sorting and Selecting Data

Data files are not always organized in the ideal form for your specific needs. To prepare data for analysis, you can select from a wide range of file transformations, including the ability to:

- **Sort data**. You can sort cases based on the value of one or more variables.
- **Select subsets of cases**. You can restrict your analysis to a subset of cases or perform simultaneous analyses on different subsets.

## Sorting Data

Sorting cases (sorting rows of the data file) is often useful—and sometimes necessary—for certain types of analysis. To reorder the sequence of cases in the data file based on the value of one or more sorting variables, from the menus choose:

Data
  Sort Cases...

This opens the Sort Cases dialog box, as shown in Figure 13.1.

**Figure 13.1   Sort Cases dialog box**

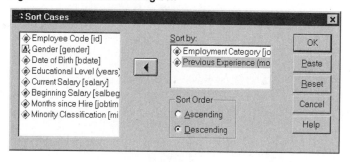

If you select multiple sort variables, the order in which they appear on the Sort By list determines the order in which cases are sorted. For example, based on

119

the Sort By list in Figure 13.1, cases will be sorted by the value of *prevexp* within categories of *jobcat*. For string variables, uppercase letters precede their lowercase counterparts in sort order (for example, the string value Yes comes before yes in sort order).

## Split-File Processing

To split your data file into separate groups for analysis, from the menus choose:

Data
  Split File...

This opens the Split File dialog box, as shown in Figure 13.2.

**Figure 13.2    Split File dialog box**

*The Split File procedure automatically sorts the data file based on the values of the grouping variables. If the original order of cases is important, do not save the file after using the Split File option.*

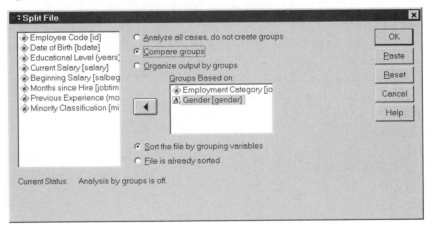

To split the data file into separate groups for analysis:

1. Select Compare groups or Organize output by groups.

2. Select the variable(s) to use to split the file into separate groups.

You can use numeric, short string, and long string variables as grouping variables. A separate analysis is performed for each subgroup defined by the grouping variables. If you select multiple grouping variables, the order in which they appear on the Groups Based On list determines the manner in which cases are grouped. For example, based on the Groups Based On list in Figure 13.2, cases will be grouped by the value of *gender* within categories of *jobcat*.

### Sorting Cases for Split-File Processing

The Split File procedure creates a new subgroup each time it encounters a different value for one of the grouping variables. Therefore, it is important to sort cases based on the values of the grouping variables before invoking split-file processing.

By default, Split File automatically sorts the data file based on the values of the grouping variables. If the file is already sorted in the proper order, you can save processing time if you select File is already sorted.

### Turning Split-File Processing On and Off

*You can easily reopen the Split File dialog box by clicking on*

Once you invoke split-file processing, it remains in effect for the rest of the session unless you turn it off.

- **Analyze all cases.** Turns split-file processing off.
- **Compare groups** and **Organize output by groups.** Turns split-file processing on.

If split-file processing is in effect, the message Split File on appears on the status bar at the bottom of the application window.

## Selecting Subsets of Cases

You can restrict your analysis to a specific subgroup based on criteria that include variables and complex expressions. You can also select a random sample of cases. The criteria used to define a subgroup can include:

- Variable values and ranges
- Date and time ranges
- Case (row) numbers
- Arithmetic expressions
- Logical expressions
- Functions

To select a subset of cases for analysis, from the menus choose:

Data
  Select Cases...

This opens the Select Cases dialog box, as shown in Figure 13.3.

**Figure 13.3    Select Cases dialog box**

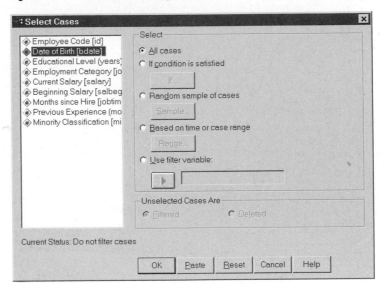

## Unselected Cases

*If you delete unselected cases and save the file, the cases cannot be recovered.*

You can choose one of the following alternatives for the treatment of unselected cases:

- **Filtered**. Unselected cases are not included in the analysis but remain in the data file. You can use the unselected cases later in the session if you turn filtering off. If you select a random sample or if you select cases based on a conditional expression, this generates a variable named *filter_$* with a value of 1 for selected cases and a value of 0 for unselected cases.

- **Deleted**. Unselected cases are deleted from the data file. By reducing the number of cases in the open data file, you can save processing time. Deleted cases can be recovered only by exiting from the file without saving any changes and then reopening the file. The deletion of cases is permanent if you save the changes to the data file.

## Selecting Cases Based on Conditional Expressions

To select cases based on a conditional expression, select If condition is satisfied and click If in the Select Cases dialog box. This opens the Select Cases If dialog box, as shown in Figure 13.4.

**Figure 13.4    Select Cases If dialog box**

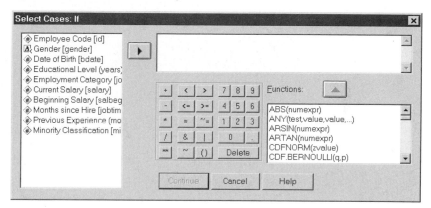

The conditional expression can use existing variable names, constants, arithmetic operators, logical operators, relational operators, and functions. You can type and edit the expression in the text box just like text in an output window (see Chapter 4). You can also use the calculator pad, variable list, and function list to paste elements into the expression. See Chapter 12 for more information on working with conditional expressions.

## Selecting a Random Sample

To obtain a random sample, select Random sample of cases in the Select Cases dialog box and click Sample. This opens the Select Cases Random Sample dialog box, as shown in Figure 13.5.

**Figure 13.5    Select Cases Random Sample dialog box**

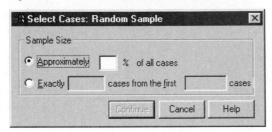

**Sample Size**. You can select one of the following alternatives for sample size:

- **Approximately**. A user-specified percentage. This option generates a random sample of approximately the specified percentage of cases.

- **Exactly**. A user-specified number of cases. You must also specify the number of cases from which to generate the sample. This second number should be less than or equal to the total number of cases in the data file. If the number exceeds the total number of cases in the data file, the sample will contain proportionally fewer cases than the requested number.

## Selecting a Time Range or Case Range

To select a range of cases based on dates, times, or observation (row) number, select **Based on time or case range** and click **Range** in the Select Cases dialog box. This opens the Select Cases Range dialog box, as shown on the left in Figure 13.6. For time series data with defined date variables, you can select a range of dates and/or times based on the defined date variables, as shown on the right in Figure 13.6. For other data files, you can select a range of observation (row) numbers. To generate date variables for time series data, use the Define Dates option on the Data menu.

**Figure 13.6    Select Cases Range dialog boxes**

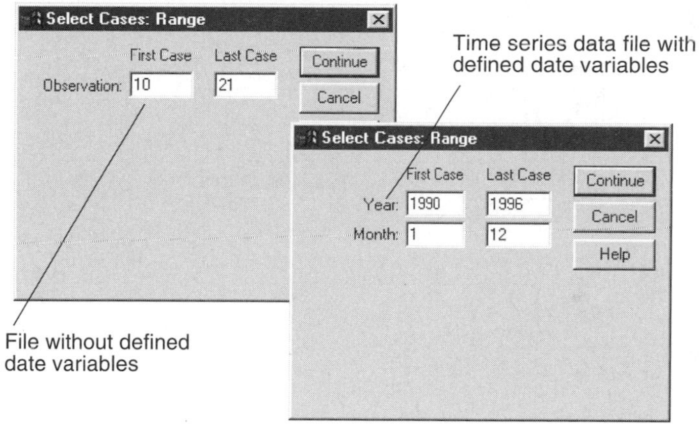

*In a time series data file, each case represents observations at a different time, and the file is sorted in chronological order. To define date variables for time series data, use the Define Dates option on the Data menu.*

**First Case**. Enter the starting date and/or time values for the range. If no date variables are defined, enter the starting observation number (row number in the Data Editor, unless Split File is on). If you do not specify a Last Case value, all cases from the starting date/time to the end of the time series are selected.

**Last Case**. Enter the ending date and/or time values for the range. If no date variables are defined, enter the ending observation number (row number in the Data Editor, unless Split File is on). If you do not specify a First Case value, all cases from the beginning of the time series up to the ending date/time are selected.

# Case Selection Status

If you have selected a subset of cases but have not discarded unselected cases, unselected cases are marked in the Data Editor with a diagonal line through the row number, as shown in Figure 13.7.

**Figure 13.7    Case selection status**

Unselected
(excluded)
cases

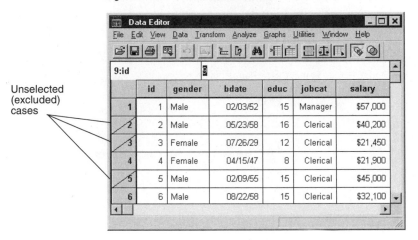

# 14

## Additional Statistical Procedures

This chapter contains brief tutorials for selected statistical procedures. It also refers to other chapters in this manual where other procedures are shown. The procedures are grouped according to the order in which they appear on the Analyze menu.

The examples are designed to illustrate sample specifications required to run a statistical procedure. Most of the examples use the *Employee data.sav* file, which is described in Chapter 4. The exponential smoothing example uses the *Inventor.sav* file, which contains inventory data collected over a period of 70 days. In the examples in this chapter, you must run the procedures to see the output.

For information about individual items in a dialog box, click Help. If you want to locate a specific statistic, such as percentiles, use the Search facility in the Help system, which is described in Chapter 2. For additional information about interpreting the results obtained by running these procedures, consult a statistics or data analysis textbook.

## Summarize Data

The Descriptive Statistics submenu on the Analyze menu provides techniques for summarizing data with statistics and charts. The following are brief tutorials for the Frequencies and Explore procedures.

### Frequencies

An example showing a frequency table and a bar chart is provided in Chapter 1. In that example, the Frequencies procedure was used to analyze the variable *jobcat*, which has a small number of distinct job categories. If the variable you want to analyze has a large number of different values, you can use the Frequencies procedure to generate summary statistics and a histogram. A **histogram** is a chart that shows the number of cases in each of several groups. To generate statistics and a histogram of the current salaries in the *Employee data.sav* file, follow these steps:

**❶** From the menus choose:

Analyze
  Descriptive Statistics
    Frequencies...

This opens the Frequencies dialog box, as shown in Figure 14.1.

**Figure 14.1   Frequencies dialog box**

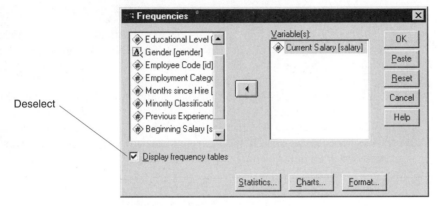

Deselect

**❷** Select *Current Salary* as a variable.

**❸** Click Charts to open the Frequencies Charts dialog box, as shown in Figure 14.2.

**Figure 14.2   Frequencies Charts dialog box**

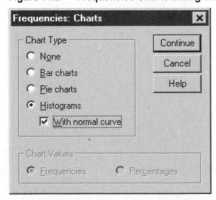

**❹** Select Histograms and With normal curve, and then click Continue.

**❺** To select summary statistics, click Statistics in the Frequencies dialog box. Select Mean, Std. deviation, and Maximum in the Frequencies Statistics dialog box, and then click Continue.

**❻** Deselect Display frequency tables in the main Frequencies dialog box.

(If you leave this item selected and display a frequency table for current salary, the output shows an entry for every distinct value of salary, making a very long table.)

**❼** Click OK to run the procedure.

The Viewer shows the requested statistics and a histogram in standard graphics format. Each bar in the histogram represents the number of employees within a salary range, and the salary values displayed are the range midpoints. As requested, a normal curve is superimposed on the chart.

## Explore

Suppose you want to look further at the distribution of salary for each job category in the *Employee data.sav* file. With the Explore procedure, you can examine the distribution of salary within categories of another variable.

**❶** From the menus choose:

Analyze
  Descriptive Statistics
    Explore...

This opens the Explore dialog box, as shown in Figure 14.3.

**Figure 14.3    Explore dialog box**

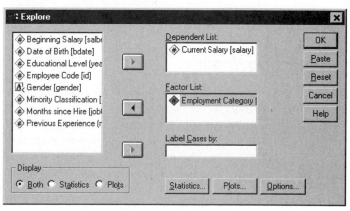

**❷** Select *Current Salary* for the Dependent List.

③ Select *Employee Category* for the Factor List.

④ Click OK to run the Explore procedure.

In the output, descriptive statistics and a stem-and-leaf plot are displayed for the current salaries in each job category. The Viewer also contains a boxplot (in standard graphics format) comparing the salaries in the job categories. For each category, the boxplot shows the median, interquartile range (25th to 75th percentile), outliers (indicated by O), and extreme values (indicated by *).

## More about Summarizing Data

There are many ways to summarize data. For example, to calculate medians or percentiles, use the Frequencies procedure or the Explore procedure. The following lists some additional methods:

- **Descriptives.** For current salary, you can calculate standard scores, sometimes called $z$ **scores**. Use the Descriptives procedure and select Save standardized values as variables.

- **Crosstabs.** Instead of making one table, as in the example of the Crosstabs procedure in Chapter 4, you can create separate tables for males and females by moving *Gender* into the layer box and selecting *Minority Classification* as the column variable.

- **Summarize procedure.** You can use the Summarize procedure to write to your output window a listing of the actual values of gender, job category, and current salary of the first 25 or 50 employees. To run the Summarize procedure, from the menus choose:

Analyze
 Reports
  Case Summaries...

# Comparing Means

The Compare Means submenu on the Analyze menu provides techniques for displaying descriptive statistics and testing whether differences are significant between two means for both independent and paired samples. You can also test whether differences are significant among more than two independent means by using the One-Way ANOVA procedure. The following tutorials use two procedures from this group, Means and Paired-Samples T Test.

## Means

In the employee data file, several variables are available for dividing the employees into groups. You can then calculate various statistics in order to compare the groups. For example, you can compute the average (mean) salaries for minority and nonminority males and females. To calculate the means, use the following steps:

❶ From the menus choose:

Analyze
  Compare Means
    Means...

This opens the Means dialog box, as shown in Figure 14.4.

**Figure 14.4    Means dialog box (layer 1)**

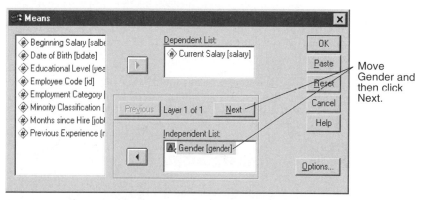

❷ Select *Current Salary* for the Dependent List.

❸ Select *Gender* for the Independent List in layer 1.

❹ Click Next. This creates another layer, as shown in Figure 14.5.

**Figure 14.5    Means dialog box (layer 2)**

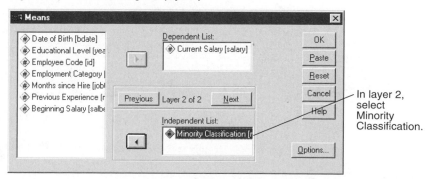

⑤ Select *Minority Classification* for the Independent List in layer 2.

⑥ Click OK to run the procedure.

## Paired-Samples T Test

When the data are structured in such a way that there are two observations on the same individual or observations that are matched by another variable on two individuals (twins, for example), the samples are paired. In the employee data file, a beginning salary and a current salary are listed for each employee. If the company is prospering, periodic raises would probably be granted, and you would certainly expect that the average current salary is greater than the average beginning salary.

To carry out a *t* test of the beginning salary and current salary means, use the following steps:

① From the menus choose:

Analyze
  Compare Means
    Paired-Samples T Test...

This opens the Paired-Samples T Test dialog box, as shown in Figure 14.6.

Figure 14.6    Paired-Samples T Test dialog box

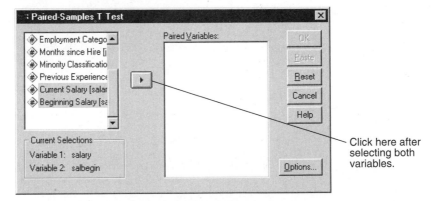

② Click *salary*. The variable is displayed in the Current Selections group.

③ Click *salbegin*. The variable is displayed in the Current Selections group.

④ Click the arrow button to move the pair to the Paired Variables list.

⑤ Click OK to run the procedure.

**❻** If there are rows of asterisks in some columns, double-click the chart and drag the columns wider.

The results, as expected, show that the current salary is significantly different from the beginning salary, as indicated by the small probability displayed in the *Sig. (2-tailed)* column of the Paired Samples Test table. The data structure in this example is similar to an experiment in which the same person is observed before and after an intervention.

## More about Comparing Means

The following examples suggest some ways in which you can use other procedures to compare means.

- **Independent-Samples T Test.** When you use a *t* test to compare means of one variable across independent groups, the samples are independent. Males and females in the employee file can be divided into independent groups by the variable *Gender*. You can use a *t* test to determine if the mean current salaries of males and females are the same.

- **One-Sample T Test.** You can test whether the average salary of clerical workers in this company differs from a national or state average. Use Select Cases on the Data menu to select the cases with *Employment Category* = 1. Then, run the One-Sample T Test procedure to compare *Current Salary* and the test value 35000.

- **One-Way ANOVA.** The variable *Employment Category* divides employees into three independent groups by employment category. You can use the One-Way ANOVA procedure to test whether mean beginning salaries for the three groups are significantly different.

# ANOVA Models

The General Linear Model submenu on the Analyze menu provides techniques for testing univariate analysis-of-variance models. (If you have only one factor, you can use the One-Way ANOVA procedure on the Compare Means submenu.)

## Univariate Analysis of Variance

The GLM Univariate procedure can perform an analysis of variance for factorial designs. A simple factorial design can be used to test if employees with differing minority and gender classifications have the same beginning salaries.

❶ From the menus choose:

Analyze
  General Linear Model
    Univariate...

This opens the Univariate dialog box, as shown in Figure 14.7.

**Figure 14.7    Univariate dialog box**

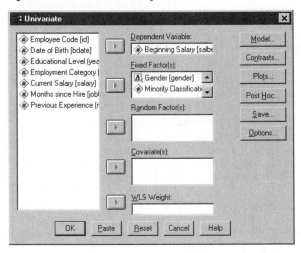

❷ Select *Beginning Salary* as the dependent variable.

❸ Select *Gender* and *Minority Classification* as fixed factors.

❹ Click OK to run the procedure.

In the Tests of Between Subjects Effects table, you can see that the effects of *Gender* and *Minority Classification* are definitely significant and that the observed significance level of the interaction of *Gender* and *Minority* is 0.014. For further interpretation, consult a statistics or data analysis textbook.

## Correlating Variables

The Correlate submenu on the Analyze menu provides measures of association for two or more numeric variables. Following are an example of the Bivariate Correlations procedure and a brief tutorial using the Partial Correlations procedure.

## Bivariate Correlations

The Bivariate Correlations procedure computes statistics such as Pearson's correlation coefficient. Correlations measure how variables or rank orders are related. Correlation coefficients range in value from –1 (a perfect negative relationship) and +1 (a perfect positive relationship). A value of 0 indicates no linear relationship.

For example, you can use Pearson's correlation coefficient to see if there is a strong linear association between *salary* (current salary) and *salbegin* (beginning salary).

## Partial Correlations

The Partial Correlations procedure calculates partial correlation coefficients that describe the relationship between two variables while adjusting for the effects of one or more additional variables.

You can estimate the correlation between *salbegin* and *salary*, controlling for the linear effects of *jobtime* (time on the job) and *prevexp* (previous experience). The number of control variables determines the order of the partial correlation coefficient.

**1** From the menus choose:

Analyze
 Correlate
  Partial...

This opens the Partial Correlations dialog box, as shown in Figure 14.8.

**Figure 14.8    Partial Correlations dialog box**

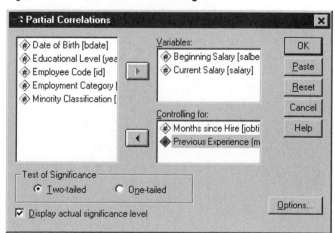

**②** Select *Beginning Salary* and *Current Salary* as variables.

**③** Select *Months since Hire* and *Previous Experience* as control variables.

**④** Click OK to run the procedure.

The output shows a table of partial correlation coefficients, the degrees of freedom, and the significance level for the pair *salary* and *salbegin*.

# Regression Analysis

The Regression submenu on the Analyze menu provides regression techniques, including curve estimation. Following is a brief tutorial using the Linear Regression procedure.

## Linear Regression

The Linear Regression procedure examines the relationship between a dependent variable and a set of independent variables. You can use it to predict an employee's current salary (the dependent variable) from independent variables such as number of years of education, months of experience, gender, and minority classification.

**①** From the menus choose:

Analyze
  Regression
    Linear...

This opens the Linear Regression dialog box, as shown in Figure 14.9.

**Figure 14.9    Linear Regression dialog box**

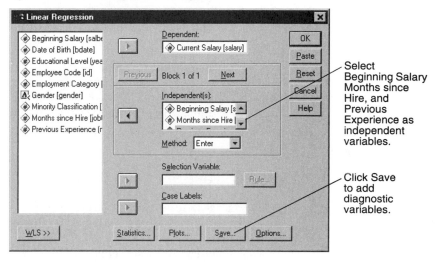

Select Beginning Salary Months since Hire, and Previous Experience as independent variables.

Click Save to add diagnostic variables.

**❷** Select *Current Salary* as the dependent variable.

**❸** Select *Beginning Salary*, *Months since Hire*, and *Previous Experience* as the independent variables.

**❹** Click OK to run the procedure.

The output contains goodness-of-fit statistics and the partial regression coefficients for the variables.

**Examining fit.** To see how well the regression model fits your data, you can examine the residuals and other types of diagnostics that this procedure provides. In the Linear Regression dialog box, click Save to see a list of the new variables you can add to your data file. If you generate any of these variables, they will not be available in a later session unless you save the data file.

**Methods.** If you have collected a large number of independent variables and want to build a regression model that includes only variables that are statistically related to the dependent variable, you can select a method from the drop-down list. For example, if you select Stepwise in the above example, only variables that meet the criteria in the Linear Regression Options dialog box are entered in the equation.

## More about Regression Procedures

The following example uses another regression procedure:

- **Curve Estimation.** You can use the Curve Estimation procedure to fit linear, quadratic, and cubic models of *Current Salary* as a function of *Beginning Salary*.

To use the Curve Estimation procedure for predictions for time series data, in the Independent group, select Time and then click Save. Select Predicted values and Predict through. Make entries in the Curve Estimation Save dialog box similar to the entries described for prediction in "Exponential Smoothing" on p. 140.

# Nonparametric Tests

The Nonparametric Tests submenu on the Analyze menu provides nonparametric tests for one sample or for two or more paired or independent samples. Nonparametric tests do not require assumptions about the shape of the distributions from which the data originate. Following is a brief tutorial using the Chi-Square Test procedure.

## Chi-Square

The Chi-Square Test procedure is used to test hypotheses about the relative proportion of cases falling into several mutually exclusive groups. You can test the hypothesis that employees in the company occur in the same proportions of gender as the general population (50% males, 50% females).

In this example, you will need to recode the string variable *Gender* into a numeric variable before you can run the procedure.

**1** From the menus choose:

Transform
  Automatic Recode...

This opens the Automatic Recode dialog box, as shown in Figure 14.10.

**Figure 14.10    Automatic Recode dialog box**

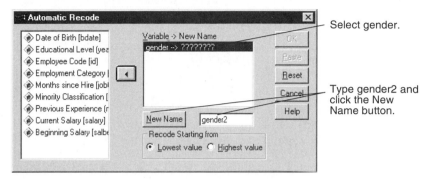

② Select the variable *Gender* and move it into the Variable –> New Name list.

③ Type *gender2* in the New Name text box, and then click the **New Name** button.

④ Click **OK** to run the procedure.

This creates a new numeric variable called *gender2,* which has a value of 1 for females and a value of 2 for males. Now a chi-square test can be run with a numeric variable.

① From the menus choose:

Analyze
  Nonparametric Tests
    Chi-Square...

This opens the Chi-Square Test dialog box, as shown in Figure 14.11.

**Figure 14.11    Chi-Square Test dialog box**

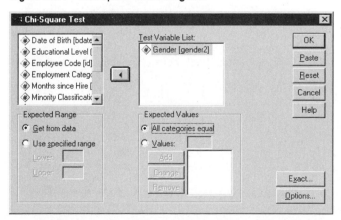

**2** Select *Gender [gender2]* as the test variable.

**3** Select All categories equal, since, in the general population of working age, the number of males and females is approximately equal.

**4** Click OK to run the procedure.

The output shows a table of the expected and residual values for the categories. The significance of the chi-square test is slightly above 0.05. Consult a statistics or data analysis text book for more information on interpretation of the statistics.

# Time Series Analysis

A **time series variable** is a variable whose values are recorded at regular intervals over a period of time. The Time Series submenu on the Analyze menu provides exponential smoothing that can be used for predictions. Following is a brief tutorial using the Exponential Smoothing procedure. Exponential Smoothing is available in the Student Version and in the Trends module.

## Exponential Smoothing

The Exponential Smoothing procedure performs exponential smoothing of time series data. It creates new series containing predicted values and residuals.

For example, you can fit a model for inventory data and use it to predict the next week's inventory. Suppose that for 70 days you have kept track of the inventory of power supplies and that you want to construct a model and then use it to forecast power supplies for the next week.

**1** Open the *Inventor.sav* file. It is usually in the directory where SPSS is installed. If the file is not available, see the preface.

**2** From the menus choose:

Analyze
  Time Series
    Exponential Smoothing...

This opens the Exponential Smoothing dialog box, as shown in Figure 14.12.

**Figure 14.12    Exponential Smoothing dialog box**

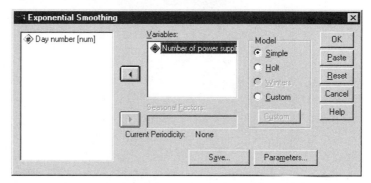

❸ Select *Number of power supplies* for the Variables list.

❹ Click Parameters to specify the procedure.

This opens the Exponential Smoothing Parameters dialog box, as shown in Figure 14.13.

**Figure 14.13    Exponential Smoothing Parameters dialog box**

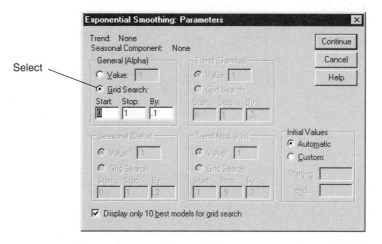

❺ To search for the best general parameter, select Grid Search and then click Continue.

❻ To create a new variable that contains predicted values, click Save.

This opens the Exponential Smoothing Save dialog box, as shown in Figure 14.14.

**Figure 14.14    Exponential Smoothing Save dialog box**

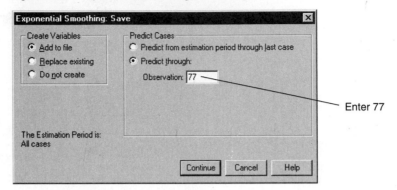

**7** Select **Predict through** and type **77** in the Observation text box.

This adds 7 days to the original 70.

**8** Click **Continue** and then in the main dialog box, click **OK**.

This runs the procedure and adds the new variables *fit_1* and *err_1*. The variable *fit_1* contains the fitted values and the seven new predicted values. The variable *err_1* contains residual values for the original 70 cases; you can use the residuals for further analysis. If you want to save the new variables, select **Save As** from the File menu and save the data file under a new name.

**9** To see a chart of the original data and the new fit line, from the menus choose:

Graphs
  Sequence...

This opens the Sequence Charts dialog box, as shown in Figure 14.15.

**Figure 14.15    Sequence Charts dialog box**

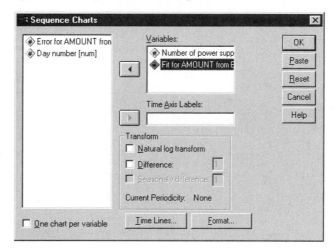

⑩ Select *Number of power supplies* and *Fit for AMOUNT* as variables.

⑪ Click OK to run the procedure.

The resulting chart shows both the actual number of power supplies and the fit line plotted on the same axes. The predicted values are plotted for the next week at the right side of the chart.

# Tutorial: Creating Standard Bar Charts

This tutorial introduces the basics of creating standard (non-interactive) charts using the Graphs menu and demonstrates the following:

- Creating a simple bar chart summarizing groups of cases
- Creating a simple bar chart summarizing separate variables
- Creating a clustered bar chart

This tutorial uses the file *Employee data.sav*, described in previous chapters. If you need help in opening the file, see Chapter 4. For interactive bar charts, see Chapter 6.

# Creating a Chart Summarizing Groups of Cases

Figure A.1 shows a simple bar chart that plots the mean salary for employees within each job category.

**Figure A.1   Simple bar chart**

*A single categorical variable (jobcat) is summarized. Each bar represents the mean Current Salary for a group of cases.*

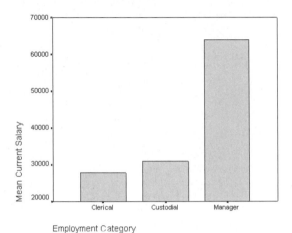

① To create the above bar chart, from the menus choose:

Graphs
  Bar...

This opens the Bar Charts dialog box, as shown in Figure A.2.

**Figure A.2   Bar Charts dialog box**

Already
selected

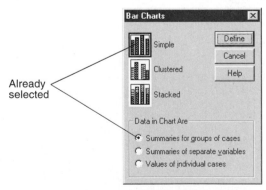

The option for a simple bar chart should already be selected, as well as the option Summaries for groups of cases, which is used to summarize a variable within categories.

❷ Click Define.

This opens the Define Simple Bar Summaries for Groups of Cases dialog box, as shown in Figure A.3.

**Figure A.3    Define Simple Bar Summaries for Groups of Cases dialog box**

*Each bar will represent the mean current salary within a single job category.*

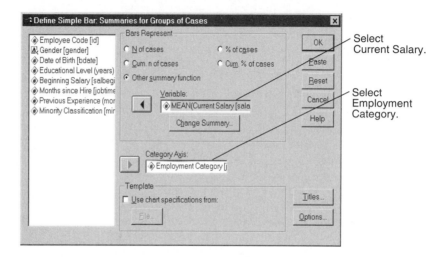

Select Current Salary.

Select Employment Category.

❸ In the Bars Represent group, select Other summary function. Select *Current Salary* for the summary function variable.

MEAN(Current Salary) appears in the Variable box.

❹ Select *Employment Category* for Category Axis.

There will be a separate bar for each job category.

❺ Click OK.

The chart is displayed in the Viewer, as shown in Figure A.4.

**Figure A.4    Simple bar chart in the Viewer**

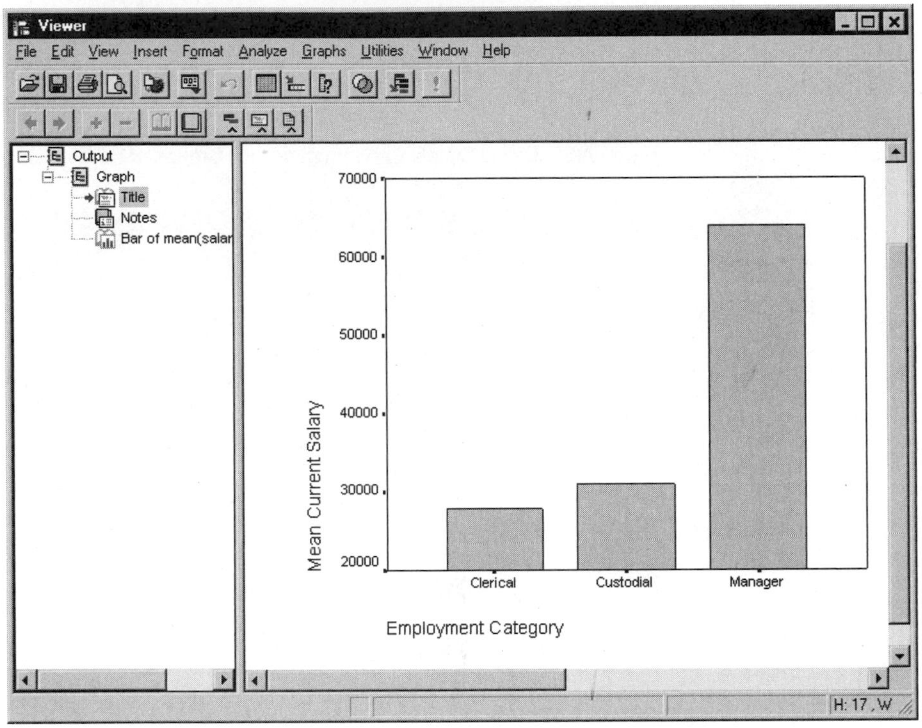

# Creating a Chart Summarizing Separate Variables

Suppose you now want to compare beginning and current salaries. You can create a bar chart that shows mean current and beginning salaries for all employees. The capability of summarizing separate variables as categories in a chart is available only for standard charts.

❶ From the menus choose:

Graphs
   Bar...

This opens the Bar Charts dialog box, as shown in Figure A.5.

**Figure A.5    Bar Charts dialog box**

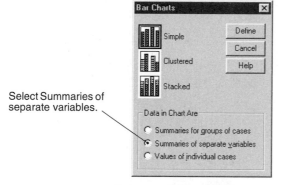

Select Summaries of
separate variables.

❷ In the Data in Chart Are group, select Summaries of separate variables.

❸ Click Define.

This opens the Define Simple Bar Summaries of Separate Variables dialog box, as shown in Figure A.6.

**Figure A.6    Define Simple Bar Summaries of Separate Variables dialog box**

*Each bar will represent the mean of a separate variable across all cases.*

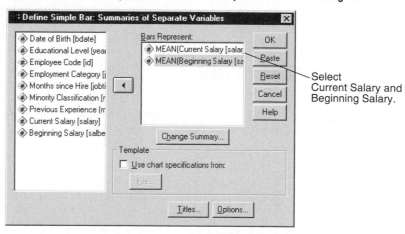

Select
Current Salary and
Beginning Salary.

❹ Select *Current Salary* on the variable list and click the arrow button.

MEAN(Current Salary) appears on the Bars Represent list.

❺ Select *Beginning Salary* and click the arrow button again.

MEAN(Beginning Salary) appears on the Bars Represent list.

⑥ Click OK.

The chart is displayed in the Viewer (see Figure A.7).

**Figure A.7    Bar chart of Current Salary and Beginning Salary in the Viewer**

*Each bar represents the mean of a separate variable.*

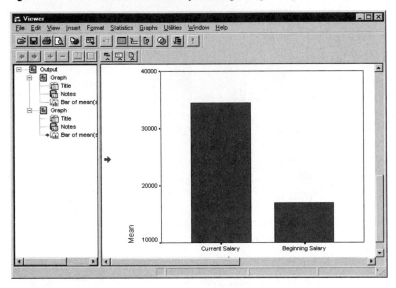

## Creating a Clustered Bar Chart

In a clustered bar chart, there is a cluster of bars (rather than a single bar) for each point on the category axis. Figure A.8 shows a clustered bar chart that plots the number of males and females within each job category.

**Figure A.8    Clustered bar chart**

*There is a cluster of bars for each point on the category axis.*

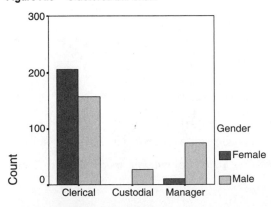

To create the clustered bar chart shown above:

**1** From the menus choose:

Graphs
  Bar...

This opens the Bar Charts dialog box, as shown in Figure A.9.

**Figure A.9    Bar Charts dialog box**

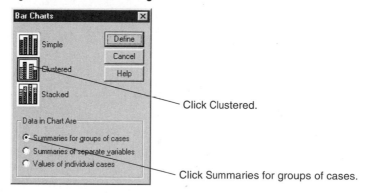

**2** To create a clustered bar chart, click Clustered.

**3** In the Data in Chart Are group, select Summaries for groups of cases.

In this example, cases are first grouped according to job category and then further grouped within each job category according to gender.

**4** Click Define.

This opens the Define Clustered Bar Summaries for Groups of Cases dialog box, as shown in Figure A.10.

**Figure A.10    Define Clustered Bar Summaries for Groups of Cases dialog box**

*Categories of gender will be summarized within categories of jobcat.*

Select Employment Category.

Select Gender.

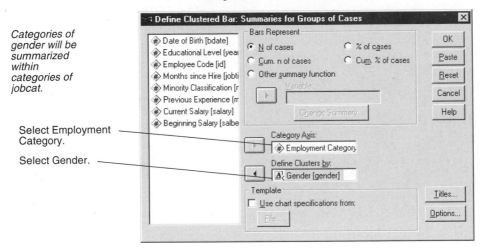

In the Bars Represent group, the default N of cases will chart the number of cases in each of the categories.

**❺** Select *Employment Category* for Category Axis.

There will be a separate cluster of bars for each job category.

**❻** Select *gender* for Define Clusters By.

Within each cluster, there will be a separate bar for males and females.

**❼** Click OK.

Figure A.11 shows the resulting chart.

**Figure A.11   Clustered bar chart in the Viewer**

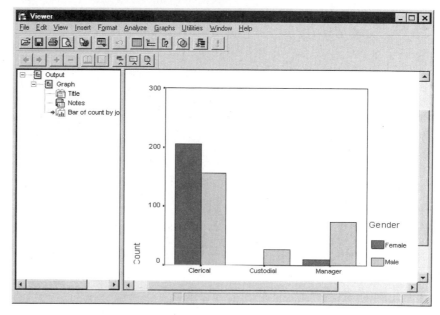

# Pasting Standard Charts into Another Application

To copy and paste a standard chart into another application, such as a word-processing program:

1. Select the chart in the Viewer (click on the chart once to select it).

2. From the menus choose:

    Edit
      Copy

    This copies the chart to the Windows clipboard in metafile and bitmap format.

3. Position the cursor in the target application where you want to place the chart.

4. From the target application's menus choose:

    Edit
      Paste Special...

5. From the Paste Special dialog box, select Picture or Bitmap.

## What's Next?

At this point, you can choose to continue experimenting with the Graphs menu, continue with the next tutorial (where you will learn how to edit standard charts), or exit the program. If you exit, do *not* save any changes to the *Employee data.sav* file.

# Tutorial: Creating and Modifying a Standard Scatterplot

This tutorial introduces the basics of editing standard (non-interactive) charts in a chart window and demonstrates the following:

- Creating a scatterplot
- Moving the scatterplot from the Viewer into a chart window
- Using point selection mode to identify points in the scatterplot
- Changing the scale of the *x* axis
- Adding a regression line and title to the scatterplot

This tutorial uses the file *Employee data.sav*, described in previous chapters. If you need help in opening the file, see Chapter 4. For interactive scatterplots, see Chapter 7.

## Creating a Scatterplot

A scatterplot shows the relationship between two continuous variables, such as *Current Salary* and *Beginning Salary*.

**1** To create a scatterplot that shows the relationship between beginning and current salary, from the menus choose:

Graphs
  Scatter...

This opens the Scatterplot dialog box, as shown in Figure B.1. (The Simple chart type is selected by default.)

**Figure B.1    Scatterplot dialog box**

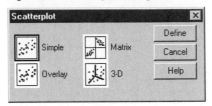

**2** Click Define.

This opens the Simple Scatterplot dialog box, as shown in Figure B.2.

**Figure B.2    Simple Scatterplot dialog box**

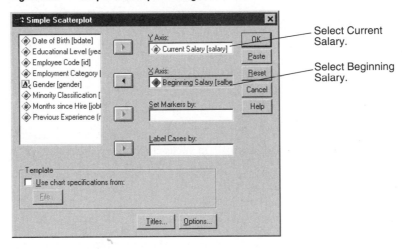

**3** Select *Current Salary* for the *y* axis and select *Beginning Salary* for the *x* axis.

**4** Click OK.

The chart is displayed in the Viewer, as shown in Figure B.3.

**Figure B.3    Scatterplot in the Viewer**

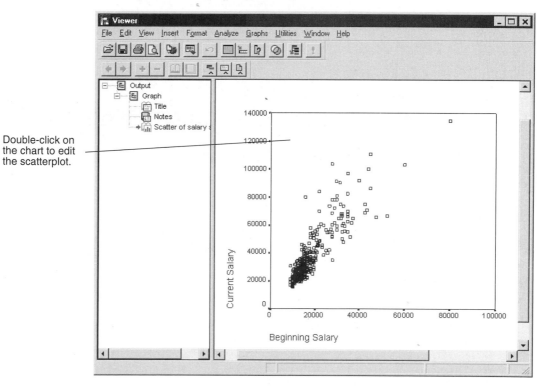

Double-click on
the chart to edit
the scatterplot.

## Editing the Chart

*You can have
more than one
Chart Editor
window open at
one time. Each
chart is
displayed in a
separate
window.*

To modify the chart:

**1** Double-click the chart in the Viewer. This opens a Chart Editor window containing the scatterplot, as shown in Figure B.4, with the Chart Editor menu bar and toolbar displayed.

**Figure B.4    Scatterplot in a chart window**

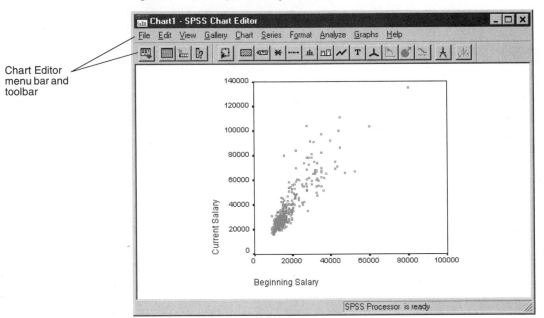

Chart Editor
menu bar and
toolbar

## Using Point Selection Mode to Identify Points

Examining your scatterplot, you notice one person whose salary has increased from roughly $30,000 to more that $100,000 (as indicated in Figure B.5). To find out more about this individual, you can use point selection mode.

**Figure B.5    Point selection mode in the chart window**

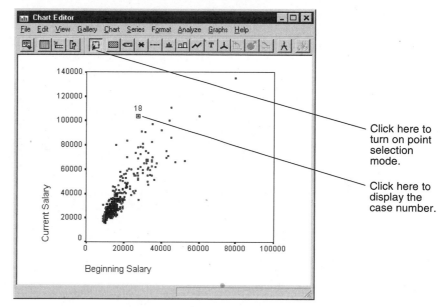

With a boxplot
or scatterplot
in the active
chart window,
click

.

The cursor
changes to

,

which
indicates
that point
selection
is on.

❶ Click ▉ on the toolbar.

This turns on point selection mode.

❷ Click on the point indicated in Figure B.5.

The value 18 is displayed, indicating that the case in question is case number 18.

❸ Click ▉ on the toolbar.

This activates the Data Editor, with case number 18 selected, as shown in Figure B.6.

**Figure B.6    Data Editor with case selected**

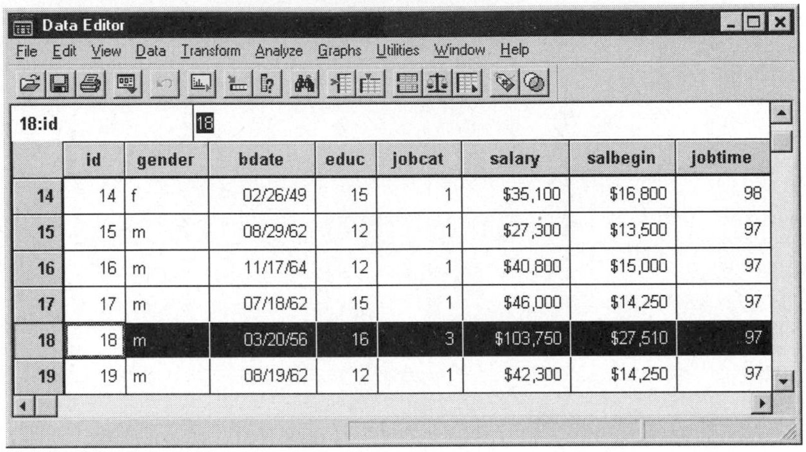

| | id | gender | bdate | educ | jobcat | salary | salbegin | jobtime |
|---|---|---|---|---|---|---|---|---|
| **14** | 14 | f | 02/26/49 | 15 | 1 | $35,100 | $16,800 | 98 |
| **15** | 15 | m | 08/29/62 | 12 | 1 | $27,300 | $13,500 | 97 |
| **16** | 16 | m | 11/17/64 | 12 | 1 | $40,800 | $15,000 | 97 |
| **17** | 17 | m | 07/18/62 | 15 | 1 | $46,000 | $14,250 | 97 |
| **18** | 18 | m | 03/20/56 | 16 | 3 | $103,750 | $27,510 | 97 |
| **19** | 19 | m | 08/19/62 | 12 | 1 | $42,300 | $14,250 | 97 |

❹ After you are finished examining the data, click 🔲 to return to the scatterplot.

❺ Click on point number 18 again to deselect it.

The displayed value 18 disappears.

❻ Click 🔲 again.

This turns off point selection mode.

## Adding a Regression Line

The scatterplot appears to be linear.

**❶** To draw a line that fits the distribution of points, from the menus choose:

Chart
  Options...

This opens the Scatterplot Options dialog box, as shown in Figure B.7.

**Figure B.7    Scatterplot Options dialog box**

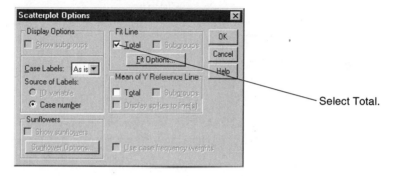

**❷** In the Fit Line group, select Total.

All of the points will be used when the position of the line is calculated.

**❸** Click OK.

This places a regression line on the scatterplot. (Figure B.10 on p. 163 shows the finished scatterplot.)

## Changing the Scale Axis

Suppose you want to see cases with beginning salaries below $40,000 in more detail. You can change the scale of the *x* axis so that only these cases are displayed.

❶ Double-click on one of the numbers in the horizontal axis (or choose Axis from the Chart menu, select X scale, and click OK).

This opens the X Scale Axis dialog box, as shown in Figure B.8.

**Figure B.8   X Scale Axis dialog box**

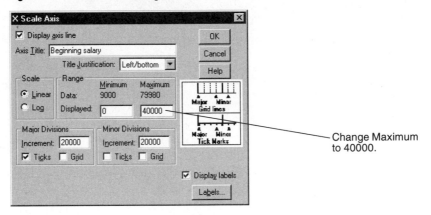

❷ In the Range text box, change the maximum displayed from 100000 to 40000, and then click OK.

Figure B.10 shows the finished scatterplot.

## Adding a Title

You can customize your chart by adding a title.

❶ To add a title to the chart, from the menus choose:

Chart
  Title...

This opens the Titles dialog box, as shown in Figure B.9.

**Figure B.9    Titles dialog box**

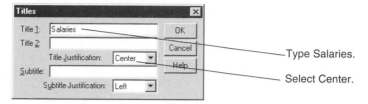

Type Salaries.
Select Center.

❷ Type **Salaries** in the Title 1 text box.

❸ To center the title, select Center from the Title Justification drop-down list.

❹ Click OK.

The title is displayed, as shown in Figure B.10.

**Figure B.10   Scatterplot with regression line, title, and modified x axis**

*Although cases with beginning salaries greater than $40,000 are not displayed, they are still used to calculate the regression line.*

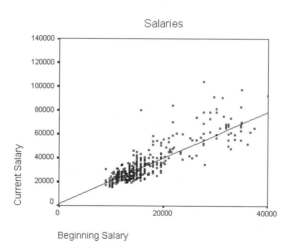

# Index